Cram101 Textbook Outlines to accompany:

Theories of Personality

Feist & Feist, 6th Edition

An Academic Internet Publishers (AIPI) publication (c) 2007.

You have a discounted membership at www.Cram101.com with this book.

Get all of the practice tests for the chapters of this textbook, and access in-depth reference material for writing essays and papers. Here is an example from a Cram101 Biology text:

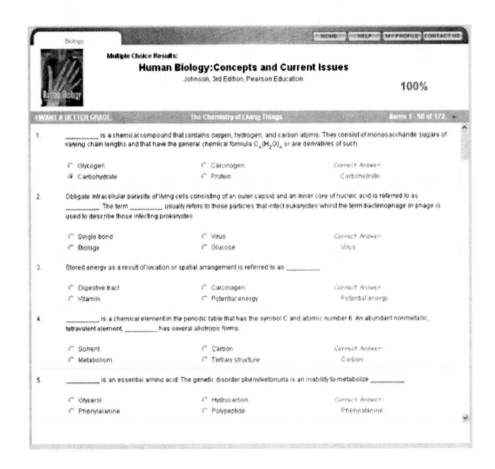

When you need problem solving help with math, stats, and other disciplines, www.Cram101.com will walk through the formulas and solutions step by step.

With Cram101.com online, you also have access to extensive reference material.

You will nail those essays and papers. Here is an example from a Cram101 Biology text:

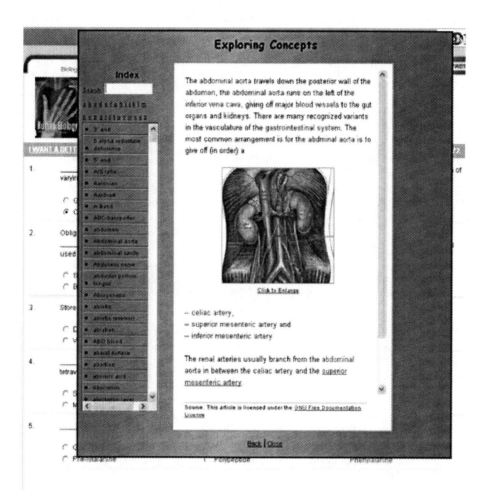

Visit **www.Cram101.com**, click Sign Up at the top of the screen, and enter DK73DW3655 in the promo code box on the registration screen. Access to www.Cram101.com is normally $9.95, but because you have purchased this book, your access fee is only $4.95. Sign up and stop highlighting textbooks forever.

Learning System

Cram101 Textbook Outlines is a learning system. The notes in this book are the highlights of your textbook, you will never have to highlight a book again.

How to use this book. Take this book to class, it is your notebook for the lecture. The notes and highlights on the left hand side of the pages follow the outline and order of the textbook. All you have to do is follow along while your intructor presents the lecture. Circle the items emphasized in class and add other important information on the right side. With Cram101 Textbook Outlines you'll spend less time writing and more time listening. Learning becomes more efficient.

Cram101.com Online

Increase your studying efficiency by using Cram101.com's practice tests and online reference material. It is the perfect complement to Cram101 Textbook Outlines. Use self-teaching matching tests or simulate in-class testing with comprehensive multiple choice tests, or simply use Cram's true and false tests for quick review. Cram101.com even allows you to enter your in-class notes for an integrated studying format combining the textbook notes with your class notes.

Visit **www.Cram101.com**, click Sign Up at the top of the screen, and enter **DK73DW3655** in the promo code box on the registration screen. Access to www.Cram101.com is normally $9.95, but because you have purchased this book, your access fee is only $4.95. Sign up and stop highlighting textbooks forever.

Theories of Personality
Feist & Feist, 6th

CONTENTS

Scientific method	Psychologists gather data in order to describe, understand, predict, and control behavior. Scientific method refers to an approach that can be used to discover accurate information. It includes these steps: understand the problem, collect data, draw conclusions, and revise research conclusions.
Sigmund Freud	Sigmund Freud was the founder of the psychoanalytic school, based on his theory that unconscious motives control much behavior, that particular kinds of unconscious thoughts and memories are the source of neurosis, and that neurosis could be treated through bringing these unconscious thoughts and memories to consciousness in psychoanalytic treatment.
Neurologist	A physician who studies the nervous system, especially its structure, functions, and abnormalities is referred to as neurologist.
Personality	Personality refers to the pattern of enduring characteristics that differentiates a person, the patterns of behaviors that make each individual unique.
Theories	Theories are logically self-consistent models or frameworks describing the behavior of a certain natural or social phenomenon. They are broad explanations and predictions concerning phenomena of interest.
Empirical	Empirical means the use of working hypotheses which are capable of being disproved using observation or experiment.
Empirical evidence	Facts or information based on direct observation or experience are referred to as empirical evidence.
Persona	In Jungian archetypal psychology, the Persona is the mask or appearance one presents to the world. It may appear in dreams under various guises.
Construct	A generalized concept, such as anxiety or gravity, is a construct.
Identical twins	Identical twins occur when a single egg is fertilized to form one zygote (monozygotic) but the zygote then divides into two separate embryos. The two embryos develop into foetuses sharing the same womb. Monozygotic twins are genetically identical unless there has been a mutation in development, and they are almost always the same gender.
Trait	An enduring personality characteristic that tends to lead to certain behaviors is called a trait. The term trait also means a genetically inherited feature of an organism.
Individuality	According to Cooper, individuality consists of two dimensions: self-assertion and separateness.
Individual differences	Individual differences psychology studies the ways in which individual people differ in their behavior. This is distinguished from other aspects of psychology in that although psychology is ostensibly a study of individuals, modern psychologists invariably study groups.
Species	Species refers to a reproductively isolated breeding population.
Temperament	Temperament refers to a basic, innate disposition to change behavior. The activity level is an important dimension of temperament.
Reasoning	Reasoning is the act of using reason to derive a conclusion from certain premises. There are two main methods to reach a conclusion, deductive reasoning and inductive reasoning.
Deductive reasoning	Deductive reasoning refers to a form of reasoning about arguments in which conclusions are determined from the premises. The conclusions are true if the premises are true.
Validity	The extent to which a test measures what it is intended to measure is called validity.
Hypothesis	A specific statement about behavior or mental processes that is testable through research is a hypothesis.
Wisdom	Wisdom is the ability to make correct judgments and decisions. It is an intangible quality gained through experience. Whether or not something is wise is determined in a pragmatic sense by its

Go to **Cram101.com** for the Practice Tests for this Chapter.

Go to **Cram101.com** for the Practice Tests for this Chapter.
And, **NEVER** highlight a book again!

	popularity, how long it has been around, and its ability to predict against future events.
Epistemology	Epistemology is the branch of philosophy that deals with the nature, origin and scope of knowledge.
Inductive reasoning	A form of reasoning in which we reason from individual cases or particular facts to a general conclusion is referred to as inductive reasoning. The conclusion can be said to follow with a probability rather than certainty.
Big five	The big five factors of personality are Openness to experience, Conscientiousness, Extraversion, Agreeableness, and Emotional Stability.
Reflection	Reflection is the process of rephrasing or repeating thoughts and feelings expressed, making the person more aware of what they are saying or thinking.
Descriptive research	Descriptive research is also known as statistical research. It describes data about the population being studied. Descriptive reseach answers the following questions: who, what, where, when and how.
Falsifiability	According to Popper the extent to which a scientific assertion is amenable to systematic probes, any one of which could negate the scientist's expectations is referred to as falsifiability.
Trial and error	Trial and error is an approach to problem solving in which one solution after another is tried in no particular order until an answer is found.
Repression	A defense mechanism, repression involves moving thoughts unacceptable to the ego into the unconscious, where they cannot be easily accessed.
Psychoanalytic	Freud's theory that unconscious forces act as determinants of personality is called psychoanalytic theory. The theory is a developmental theory characterized by critical stages of development.
Unconditional positive regard	Unqualified caring and nonjudgmental acceptance of another is called unconditional positive regard.
Empathy	Empathy is the recognition and understanding of the states of mind, including beliefs, desires and particularly emotions of others without injecting your own.
Operational definition	An operational definition is the definition of a concept or action in terms of the observable and repeatable process, procedures, and appartaus that illustrates the concept or action.
Generalization	In conditioning, the tendency for a conditioned response to be evoked by stimuli that are similar to the stimulus to which the response was conditioned is a generalization. The greater the similarity among the stimuli, the greater the probability of generalization.
Free will	The idea that human beings are capable of freely making choices or decisions is free will.
Determinism	Determinism is the philosophical proposition that every event, including human cognition and action, is causally determined by an unbroken chain of prior occurrences.
Skinner	Skinner conducted research on shaping behavior through positive and negative reinforcement, and demonstrated operant conditioning, a technique which he developed in contrast with classical conditioning.
Free choice	Free choice refers to the ability to freely make choices that are not controlled by genetics, learning, or unconscious forces.
Teleology	While science investigates natural laws and phenomena, Philosophical naturalism and teleology investigate the existence or non-existence of an organizing principle behind those natural laws and phenomena. Philosophical naturalism asserts that there are no such principles. Teleology asserts that there are.
Causation	Causation concerns the time order relationship between two or more objects such that if a specific antecendent condition occurs the same consequent must always follow.
Social influence	Social influence is when the actions or thoughts of individual(s) are changed by other individual(s).

Go to **Cram101.com** for the Practice Tests for this Chapter.

	Peer pressure is an example of social influence.
Early childhood	Early childhood refers to the developmental period extending from the end of infancy to about 5 or 6 years of age; sometimes called the preschool years.
Attention	Attention is the cognitive process of selectively concentrating on one thing while ignoring other things. Psychologists have labeled three types of attention: sustained attention, selective attention, and divided attention.
Personality inventory	A self-report questionnaire by which an examinee indicates whether statements assessing habitual tendencies apply to him or her is referred to as a personality inventory.
Reliability	Reliability means the extent to which a test produces a consistent , reproducible score .
Predictive validity	Predictive validity refers to the relation between test scores and the student 's future performance .
Construct validity	The extent to which there is evidence that a test measures a particular hypothetical construct is referred to as construct validity.
Extraversion	Extraversion, one of the big-five personailty traits, is marked by pronounced engagement with the external world. They are people who enjoy being with people, are full of energy, and often experience positive emotions.
Discriminant validity	Discriminant validity shows that a measure doesn't measure what it isn't meant to measure, it discriminates.
Convergent validity	Convergent validity measures whether a test returns similar results to other tests which purport to measure the same or related constructs.
Correlation	A statistical technique for determining the degree of association between two or more variables is referred to as correlation.
Jung	Jung was in some aspects a response to Sigmund Freud's psychoanalysis. He proposed and developed the concepts of the extroverted and introverted personality, archetypes, and the collective unconscious. His work has been influential in psychiatry and in the study of religion, literature, and related fields.
Adler	Adler argued that human personality could be explained teleologically, separate strands dominated by the guiding purpose of the individual's unconscious self ideal to convert feelings of inferiority to superiority (or rather completeness). The desires of the self ideal were countered by social and ethical demands.
Rotter	Rotter focused on the application of social learning theory (SLT) to clinical psychology. She introduced the ideas of learning from generalized expectancies of reinforcement and internal/ external locus of control (self-initiated change versus change influenced by others). According to Rotter, health outcomes could be improved by the development of a sense of personal control over one's life.
Hans Eysenck	Hans Eysenck using Factor Analysis concluded that all human traits can be broken down into two distinct categories: 1. Extroversion-Introversion, 2. Neuroticism. He called these categories Supertraits.

Learning	Learning is a relatively permanent change in behavior that results from experience. Thus, to attribute a behavioral change to learning, the change must be relatively permanent and must result from experience.
Morphine	Morphine, the principal active agent in opium, is a powerful opioid analgesic drug. According to recent research, it may also be produced naturally by the human brain. Morphine is usually highly addictive, and tolerance and physical and psychological dependence develop quickly.
Addiction	Addiction is an uncontrollable compulsion to repeat a behavior regardless of its consequences. Many drugs or behaviors can precipitate a pattern of conditions recognized as addiction, which include a craving for more of the drug or behavior, increased physiological tolerance to exposure, and withdrawal symptoms in the absence of the stimulus.
Depression	In everyday language depression refers to any downturn in mood, which may be relatively transitory and perhaps due to something trivial. This is differentiated from Clinical depression which is marked by symptoms that last two weeks or more and are so severe that they interfere with daily living.
Psychoanalytic	Freud's theory that unconscious forces act as determinants of personality is called psychoanalytic theory. The theory is a developmental theory characterized by critical stages of development.
Psychoanalytic theory	Psychoanalytic theory is a general term for approaches to psychoanalysis which attempt to provide a conceptual framework more-or-less independent of clinical practice rather than based on empirical analysis of clinical cases.
Cocaine	Cocaine is a crystalline tropane alkaloid that is obtained from the leaves of the coca plant. It is a stimulant of the central nervous system and an appetite suppressant, creating what has been described as a euphoric sense of happiness and increased energy.
Personality	Personality refers to the pattern of enduring characteristics that differentiates a person, the patterns of behaviors that make each individual unique.
Psychoanalysis	Psychoanalysis refers to the school of psychology that emphasizes the importance of unconscious motives and conflicts as determinants of human behavior. It was Freud's method of exploring human personality.
Theories	Theories are logically self-consistent models or frameworks describing the behavior of a certain natural or social phenomenon. They are broad explanations and predictions concerning phenomena of interest.
Psychodynamic	Most psychodynamic approaches are centered around the idea of a maladapted function developed early in life (usually childhood) which are at least in part unconscious. This maladapted function (a.k.a. defense mechanism) does not do well in place of a normal/healthy one.
Research method	The scope of the research method is to produce some new knowledge. This, in principle, can take three main forms: Exploratory research; Constructive research; and Empirical research.
Reasoning	Reasoning is the act of using reason to derive a conclusion from certain premises. There are two main methods to reach a conclusion, deductive reasoning and inductive reasoning.
Deductive reasoning	Deductive reasoning refers to a form of reasoning about arguments in which conclusions are determined from the premises. The conclusions are true if the premises are true.
Sigmund Freud	Sigmund Freud was the founder of the psychoanalytic school, based on his theory that unconscious motives control much behavior, that particular kinds of unconscious thoughts and memories are the source of neurosis, and that neurosis could be treated through bringing these unconscious thoughts and memories to consciousness in psychoanalytic treatment.
Friendship	The essentials of friendship are reciprocity and commitment between individuals who see

Go to **Cram101.com** for the Practice Tests for this Chapter.

Go to **Cram101.com** for the Practice Tests for this Chapter.
And, **NEVER** highlight a book again!

themselves more or less as equals. Interaction between friends rests on a more equal power base than the interaction between children and adults.

Guilt	Guilt describes many concepts related to a negative emotion or condition caused by actions which are believed to be, morally wrong. According to Freud, the avoidance of guilt is the basis for moral behavior.
Hypnosis	Hypnosis is a psychological state whose existence and effects are strongly debated. Some believe that it is a state under which the subject's mind becomes so suggestible that the hypnotist, the one who induces the state, can establish communication with the subconscious mind of the subject and command behavior that the subject would not choose to perform in a conscious state.
Free association	In psychoanalysis, the uncensored uttering of all thoughts that come to mind is called free association.
Breuer	Breuer is perhaps best known for his work with Anna O. – a woman suffering with symptoms of paralysis, anaesthesias, and disturbances of vision and speech. The discussions of Anna O. between Freud and Breuer were documented in their Studies in Hysteria and became a formative basis of Freudian theory and psychoanalytic practice.
Catharsis	Catharsis has been adopted by modern psychotherapy as the act of giving expression to deep emotions often associated with events in the individuals past which have never before been adequately expressed.
Adolescence	The period of life bounded by puberty and the assumption of adult responsibilities is adolescence.
Hysteria	Hysteria is a diagnostic label applied to a state of mind, one of unmanageable fear or emotional excesses. The fear is often centered on a body part, most often on an imagined problem with that body part.
Psychoanalyst	A psychoanalyst is a specially trained therapist who attempts to treat the individual by uncovering and revealing to the individual otherwise subconscious factors that are contributing to some undesirable behavor.
Uterus	The uterus or womb is the major female reproductive organ. The main function of the uterus is to accept a fertilized ovum which becomes implanted into the endometrium, and derives nourishment from blood vessels which develop exclusively for this purpose.
Society	The social sciences use the term society to mean a group of people that form a semi-closed (or semi-open) social system, in which most interactions are with other individuals belonging to the group.
Case study	A carefully drawn biography that may be obtained through interviews, questionnaires, and psychological tests is called a case study.
Embryonic stage	The embryonic stage lasts from the third through the eighth week following conception. During this stage the major organ systems undergo rapid differentiation.
Seduction theory	Freud believed that all hyseria was traceable to sexual seduction and abuse. This theory, known as the seduction theory, he later modified and replaced with a psychoanalytic alternative, hysteria.
Lesion	A lesion is a non-specific term referring to abnormal tissue in the body. It can be caused by any disease process including trauma (physical, chemical, electrical), infection, neoplasm, metabolic and autoimmune.
Nicotine	Nicotine is an organic compound, an alkaloid found naturally throughout the tobacco plant, with a high concentration in the leaves. It is a potent nerve poison and is included in many

insecticides. In lower concentrations, the substance is a stimulant and is one of the main factors leading to the pleasure and habit-forming qualities of tobacco smoking.

Ernest Jones	Ernest Jones was arguably the best-known follower of Freud. His writings on the subject of psychoanalysis prompted him to launch The International Journal of Psychoanalysis in 1920.
Psychosomatic	A psychosomatic illness is one with physical manifestations and perhaps a supposed psychological cause. It is often diagnosed when any known or identifiable physical cause was excluded by medical examination.
Neurosis	Neurosis, any mental disorder that, although may cause distress, does not interfere with rational thought or the persons' ability to function.
Obsession	An obsession is a thought or idea that the sufferer cannot stop thinking about. Common examples include fears of acquiring disease, getting hurt, or causing harm to someone. They are typically automatic, frequent, distressing, and difficult to control or put an end to by themselves.
Jung	Jung was in some aspects a response to Sigmund Freud's psychoanalysis. He proposed and developed the concepts of the extroverted and introverted personality, archetypes, and the collective unconscious. His work has been influential in psychiatry and in the study of religion, literature, and related fields.
Adler	Adler argued that human personality could be explained teleologically, separate strands dominated by the guiding purpose of the individual's unconscious self ideal to convert feelings of inferiority to superiority (or rather completeness). The desires of the self ideal were countered by social and ethical demands.
Psychopathology	Psychopathology refers to the field concerned with the nature and development of mental disorders.
Freudian slip	The Freudian slip is named after Sigmund Freud, who described the phenomenon he called faulty action in his 1901 book The Psychopathology of Everyday Life. The Freudian slip is an error in human action, speech or memory that is believed to be caused by the unconscious mind.
Repression	A defense mechanism, repression involves moving thoughts unacceptable to the ego into the unconscious, where they cannot be easily accessed.
Oedipus complex	The Oedipus complex is a concept developed by Sigmund Freud to explain the maturation of the infant boy through identification with the father and desire for the mother.
Ego	In Freud's view the Ego serves to balance our primitive needs and our moral beliefs and taboos. Relying on experience, a healthy Ego provides the ability to adapt to reality and interact with the outside world.
Insight	Insight refers to a sudden awareness of the relationships among various elements that had previously appeared to be independent of one another.
Masturbation	Masturbation is the manual excitation of the sexual organs, most often to the point of orgasm. It can refer to excitation either by oneself or by another, but commonly refers to such activities performed alone.
Chronic	Chronic refers to a relatively long duration, usually more than a few months.
Preconscious	In psychodynamic theory, material that is not in awareness but that can be brought into awareness by focusing one's attention is referred to as preconscious.
Instinct	Instinct is the word used to describe inherent dispositions towards particular actions. They are generally an inherited pattern of responses or reactions to certain kinds of situations.
Overt behavior	An action or response that is directly observable and measurable is an overt behavior.

Go to **Cram101.com** for the Practice Tests for this Chapter.

Mental processes	The thoughts, feelings, and motives that each of us experiences privately but that cannot be observed directly are called mental processes.
Consciousness	The awareness of the sensations, thoughts, and feelings being experienced at a given moment is called consciousness.
Blocking	If the one of the two members of a compound stimulus fails to produce the CR due to an earlier conditioning of the other member of the compound stimulus, blocking has occurred.
Analogy	An analogy is a comparison between two different things, in order to highlight some form of similarity. Analogy is the cognitive process of transferring information from a particular subject to another particular subject.
Anxiety	Anxiety is a complex combination of the feeling of fear, apprehension and worry often accompanied by physical sensations such as palpitations, chest pain and/or shortness of breath.
Castration	Castration is any action, surgical, chemical or otherwise, by which a biological male loses use of the testes. This causes sterilization, i.e. prevents him from reproducing; it also greatly reduces the production of certain hormones, such as testosterone.
Castration anxiety	Castration anxiety is a fear posited by Sigmund Freud in his writings on the Oedipus complex at the genital stage of sexual development. It asserts that boys seeing a girl's genitalia will falsely assume that the girl must have had her penis removed, probably as punishment for some misbehavior, and will be anxious lest the same happen to him.
Unconscious mind	The unconscious mind refers to information processing and brain functioning of which a person is unaware. In Freudian theory, it is the repository of unacceptable thoughts and feelings.
Perception	Perception is the process of acquiring, interpreting, selecting, and organizing sensory information.
Attention	Attention is the cognitive process of selectively concentrating on one thing while ignoring other things. Psychologists have labeled three types of attention: sustained attention, selective attention, and divided attention.
Threshold	In general, a threshold is a fixed location or value where an abrupt change is observed. In the sensory modalities, it is the minimum amount of stimulus energy necessary to elicit a sensory response.
Superego	Frued's third psychic structure, which functions as a moral guardian and sets forth high standards for behavior is the superego.
Pleasure principle	The pleasure principle is the tendency to seek pleasure and avoid pain. In Freud's theory, this principle rules the Id, but is at least partly repressed by the reality principle.
Secondary process	Secondary process is the mental activity and thinking characteristic of the ego, influenced by the demands of the environment. Characterized by organization, systematization, intellectualization, and similar processes leading to logical thought and action in adult life.
Infancy	The developmental period that extends from birth to 18 or 24 months is called infancy.
Reality principle	The reality principle tells us to subordinate pleasure to what needs to be done. Subordinating the pleasure principle to the reality principle is done through a psychological process Freud calls sublimation, where you take desires that can't be fulfilled, or shouldn't be fulfilled, and turn their energy into something useful and productive.
Early childhood	Early childhood refers to the developmental period extending from the end of infancy to about 5 or 6 years of age; sometimes called the preschool years.

Go to **Cram101.com** for the Practice Tests for this Chapter.

Go to **Cram101.com** for the Practice Tests for this Chapter.
And, **NEVER** highlight a book again!

Punishment	Punishment is the addtion of a stimulus that reduces the frequency of a response, or the removal of a stimulus that results in a reduction of the response.
Stimulus	A change in an environmental condition that elicits a response is a stimulus.
Thanatos	In psychoanalytical theory, Thanatos is the death instinct, which opposes Eros. The "death instinct" identified by Sigmund Freud, which signals a desire to give up the struggle of life and return to quiescence and the grave.
Eros	In Freudian psychology, Eros is the life instinct innate in all humans. It is the desire to create life and favours productivity and construction. Eros battles against the destructive death instinct of Thanatos.
Libido	Sigmund Freud suggested that libido is the instinctual energy or force that can come into conflict with the conventions of civilized behavior. Jung, condidered the libido as the free creative, or psychic, energy an individual has to put toward personal development, or individuation.
Genitals	Genitals refers to the internal and external reproductive organs.
Erogenous zone	An erogenous zone is an area of the human body that has heightened sensitivity and stimulation normally results in sexual response.
Sadism	Sadism is the sexual pleasure or gratification in the infliction of pain and suffering upon another person. It is considered to be a paraphilia. The word is derived from the name of the Marquis de Sade, a prolific French writer of sadistic novels.
Masochism	The counterpart of sadism is masochism, the sexual pleasure or gratification of having pain or suffering inflicted upon the self, often consisting of sexual fantasies or urges for being beaten, humiliated, bound, tortured, or otherwise made to suffer, either as an enhancement to or a substitute for sexual pleasure.
Narcissism	Narcissism is the pattern of thinking and behaving which involves infatuation and obsession with one's self to the exclusion of others.
Puberty	Puberty refers to the process of physical changes by which a child's body becomes an adult body capable of reproduction.
Sensation	Sensation is the first stage in the chain of biochemical and neurologic events that begins with the impinging of a stimulus upon the receptor cells of a sensory organ, which then leads to perception, the mental state that is reflected in statements like "I see a uniformly blue wall."
Affective	Affective is the way people react emotionally, their ability to feel another living thing's pain or joy.
Neurotic anxiety	Neurotic anxiety refers to, in psychoanalytic theory, a fear of the consequences of expressing previously punished and repressed id impulses; more generally, unrealistic fear.
Moral anxiety	In psychoanalytic theory, the ego's fear of punishment for failure to adhere to the superego's standards of proper conduct is referred to as moral anxiety.
Defense mechanism	A Defense mechanism is a set of unconscious ways to protect one's personality from unpleasant thoughts and realities which may otherwise cause anxiety. The notion is an integral part of the psychoanalytic theory.
Reaction formation	In Freud's psychoanalytic theory, reaction formation is a defense mechanism in which anxiety-producing or unacceptable emotions are replaced by their direct opposites.
Displacement	An unconscious defense mechanism in which the individual directs aggressive or sexual feelings away from the primary object to someone or something safe is referred to as

Go to **Cram101.com** for the Practice Tests for this Chapter.

Go to **Cram101.com** for the Practice Tests for this Chapter.
And, **NEVER** highlight a book again!

	displacement. Displacement in linguistics is simply the ability to talk about things not present.
Stages	Stages represent relatively discrete periods of time in which functioning is qualitatively different from functioning at other periods.
Fixation	Fixation in abnormal psychology is the state where an individual becomes obsessed with an attachment to another human, animal or inanimate object. Fixation in vision refers to maintaining the gaze in a constant direction. .
Attachment	Attachment is the tendency to seek closeness to another person and feel secure when that person is present.
Oral fixation	An oral fixation is a fixation in the oral stage of development and manifested by an obsession with stimulating the mouth, first described by Sigmund Freud.
Regression	Return to a form of behavior characteristic of an earlier stage of development is called regression.
Projection	Attributing one's own undesirable thoughts, impulses, traits, or behaviors to others is referred to as projection.
Paranoia	In popular culture, the term paranoia is usually used to describe excessive concern about one's own well-being, sometimes suggesting a person holds persecutory beliefs concerning a threat to themselves or their property and is often linked to a belief in conspiracy theories.
Mental disorder	Mental disorder refers to a disturbance in a person's emotions, drives, thought processes, or behavior that involves serious and relatively prolonged distress and/or impairment in ability to function, is not simply a normal response to some event or set of events in the person's environment.
Delusion	A false belief, not generally shared by others, and that cannot be changed despite strong evidence to the contrary is a delusion.
Homosexual	Homosexual refers to a sexual orientation characterized by aesthetic attraction, romantic love, and sexual desire exclusively for members of the same sex or gender identity.
Introjection	Introjection is a psychological process where the subject replicates in itself behaviors, attributes or other fragments of the surrounding world, especially of other subjects. Cognate concepts are identification, incorporation and internalization.
Prototype	A concept of a category of objects or events that serves as a good example of the category is called a prototype.
Latency	In child development, latency refers to a phase of psychosexual development characterized by repression of sexual impulses. In learning theory, latency is the delay between stimulus (S) and response (R), which according to Hull depends on the strength of the association.
Sublimation	Sublimation is a coping mechanism. It refers to rechanneling sexual or aggressive energy into pursuits that society considers acceptable or admirable.
Cultural values	The importance and desirability of various objects and activities as defined by people in a given culture are referred to as cultural values.
Psychosexual development	In psychodynamic theory, the process by which libidinal energy is expressed through different erogenous zones during different stages of development is called psychosexual development.
Infantile sexuality	Freud's insistence that sexuality does not begin with adolescence, that babies are sexual too, is referred to as infantile sexuality.
Ambivalence	The simultaneous holding of strong positive and negative emotional attitudes toward the same

Go to **Cram101.com** for the Practice Tests for this Chapter.

Go to **Cram101.com** for the Practice Tests for this Chapter.
And, **NEVER** highlight a book again!

situation or person is called ambivalence.

Cooing	Cooing is the spontaneous repetition of vowel sounds by infants.
Penis	The penis is the external male copulatory organ and the external male organ of urination. In humans, the penis is homologous to the female clitoris, as it develops from the same embryonic structure. It is capable of erection for use in copulation.
Phallic stage	The phallic stage is the 3rd of Freud's psychosexual stages, when awareness of and manipulation of the genitals is supposed to be a primary source of pleasure. In this stage the child deals with the Oedipus complex, if male, or the Electra Complex, if female.
Anal stage	The anal stage in psychology is the term used by Sigmund Freud to describe the development during the second year of life, in which a child's pleasure and conflict centers are in the anal area.
Oral stage	The oral stage in psychology is the term used by Sigmund Freud to describe the development during the first eighteen months of life, in which an infant's pleasure centers are in the mouth. This is the first of Freud's psychosexual stages.
Suppression	Suppression is the defense mechanism where a memory is deliberately forgotten.
Evolution	Commonly used to refer to gradual change, evolution is the change in the frequency of alleles within a population from one generation to the next. This change may be caused by different mechanisms, including natural selection, genetic drift, or changes in population (gene flow).
Denial	Denial is a psychological defense mechanism in which a person faced with a fact that is uncomfortable or painful to accept rejects it instead, insisting that it is not true despite what may be overwhelming evidence.
Reinforcement	In operant conditioning, reinforcement is any change in an environment that (a) occurs after the behavior, (b) seems to make that behavior re-occur more often in the future and (c) that reoccurence of behavior must be the result of the change.
Incest	Incest refers to sexual relations between close relatives, most often between daughter and father or between brother and sister.
Electra complex	A conflict of the phallic stage in which the girl longs for her father and resents her mother is called the Electra complex.
Anatomy	Anatomy is the branch of biology that deals with the structure and organization of living things. It can be divided into animal anatomy (zootomy) and plant anatomy (phytonomy). Major branches of anatomy include comparative anatomy, histology, and human anatomy.
Masculinity	Masculinity is a culturally determined value reflecting the set of characteristics of maleness.
Bisexuality	Bisexuality is a sexual orientation characterized by aesthetic attraction, romantic love and sexual desire for both males and females.
Femininity	Femininity is the set of characteristics defined by a culture for idealized females.
Hypothesis	A specific statement about behavior or mental processes that is testable through research is a hypothesis.
Clique	A clique is an informal and restricted social group formed by a number of people who share common. Social roles vary, but two roles commonly associated with a female clique is notably applicable to most - that of the "queen bee" and that of the "outcast".
Autoeroticism	Autoeroticism is the practice of fulfilling one's own sexual needs without a partner. The most common form of autoeroticism is masturbation.

Go to **Cram101.com** for the Practice Tests for this Chapter.

Trauma	Trauma refers to a severe physical injury or wound to the body caused by an external force, or a psychological shock having a lasting effect on mental life.
Genital stage	The genital stage in psychology is the term used by Sigmund Freud to describe the final stage of human psychosexual development. It is characterized by the expression of libido through intercourse with an adult of the other gender.
Predisposition	Predisposition refers to an inclination or diathesis to respond in a certain way, either inborn or acquired. In abnormal psychology, it is a factor that lowers the ability to withstand stress and inclines the individual toward pathology.
Repressed memory	A repressed memory, according to some theories of psychology, is a memory (often traumatic) of an event or environment which is stored by the unconscious mind but outside the awareness of the conscious mind.
Dream analysis	Dream analysis is a part of psychoanalysis that intends to look beneath the manifest content of a dream, i.e., what we perceive in the dream, to the latent content of a dream, i.e., the meaning of the dream and the reason we dreamt it.
Transference	Transference is a phenomenon in psychology characterized by unconscious redirection of feelings from one person to another.
Latent content	In psychodynamic theory, the symbolized or underlying content of dreams is called latent content.
Manifest content	In psychodynamic theory, the reported content of dreams is referred to as manifest content.
Wish fulfillment	A primitive method used by the id to attempt to gratify basic instincts is referred to as wish fulfillment.
Compulsion	An apparently irresistible urge to repeat an act or engage in ritualistic behavior such as hand washing is referred to as a compulsion.
Dream symbols	Images in dreams whose personal or emotional meanings differ from their literal meanings are called dream symbols.
Affect	A subjective feeling or emotional tone often accompanied by bodily expressions noticeable to others is called affect.
Creativity	Creativity is the ability to think about something in novel and unusual ways and come up with unique solutions to problems. It involves divergent thinking, having many solutions or views to a problem.
The Interpretation of Dreams	The Interpretation of Dreams is a book by Sigmund Freud. The book introduces the Id, the Ego, and the Superego, and describes Freud's theory of the unconscious with respect to Dream interpretation. Widely considered to be his most important contribution to Psychology.
Parapraxes	Parapraxes or Freudian slip is an error in human action, speech or memory that is believed to be caused by the unconscious mind. The error often appears to the observer as being casual, bizarre or nonsensical.
Human nature	Human nature is the fundamental nature and substance of humans, as well as the range of human behavior that is believed to be invariant over long periods of time and across very different cultural contexts.
Neuroscience	A field that combines the work of psychologists, biologists, biochemists, medical researchers, and others in the study of the structure and function of the nervous system is neuroscience.
Brain	The brain controls and coordinates most movement, behavior and homeostatic body functions such as heartbeat, blood pressure, fluid balance and body temperature. Functions of the brain

Go to **Cram101.com** for the Practice Tests for this Chapter.

are responsible for cognition, emotion, memory, motor learning and other sorts of learning. The brain is primarily made up of two types of cells: glia and neurons.

Magnetic resonance imaging	Magnetic resonance imaging is a method of creating images of the inside of opaque organs in living organisms as well as detecting the amount of bound water in geological structures. It is primarily used to demonstrate pathological or other physiological alterations of living tissues and is a commonly used form of medical imaging.
Functional magnetic resonance imaging	Functional Magnetic Resonance Imaging describes the use of MRI to measure hemodynamic signals related to neural activity in the brain or spinal cord of humans or other animals. It is one of the most recently developed forms of brain imaging.
Brain imaging	Brain imaging is a fairly recent discipline within medicine and neuroscience. Brain imaging falls into two broad categories -- structural imaging and functional imaging.
Cognition	The intellectual processes through which information is obtained, transformed, stored, retrieved, and otherwise used is cognition.
Metaphor	A metaphor is a rhetorical trope where a comparison is made between two seemingly unrelated subjects
Cognitive psychology	Cognitive psychology is the psychological science which studies the mental processes that are hypothesised to underlie behavior. This covers a broad range of research domains, examining questions about the workings of memory, attention, perception, knowledge representation, reasoning, creativity and problem solving.
Brain stem	The brain stem is the stalk of the brain below the cerebral hemispheres. It is the major route for communication between the forebrain and the spinal cord and peripheral nerves. It also controls various functions including respiration, regulation of heart rhythms, and primary aspects of sound localization.
Prefrontal cortex	The prefrontal cortex is the anterior part of the frontal lobes of the brain, lying in front of the motor and associative areas. It has been implicated in planning complex cognitive behaviors, personality expression and moderating correct social behavior. The prefrontal cortex continues to develop until around age 6.
Limbic system	The limbic system is a group of brain structures that are involved in various emotions such as aggression, fear, pleasure and also in the formation of memory. The limbic system affects the endocrine system and the autonomic nervous system. It consists of several subcortical structures located around the thalamus.
Neurotransmitter	A neurotransmitter is a chemical that is used to relay, amplify and modulate electrical signals between a neurons and another cell.
Dopamine	Dopamine is critical to the way the brain controls our movements and is a crucial part of the basal ganglia motor loop. It is commonly associated with the 'pleasure system' of the brain, providing feelings of enjoyment and reinforcement to motivate us to do, or continue doing, certain activities.
Phineas Gage	As a result of an injury to his brain, Phineas Gage reportedly had significant changes in personality and temperament, which provided some of the first evidence that specific parts of the brain, particularly the frontal lobes, might be involved in specific psychological processes dealing with emotion, personality and problem solving.
Social norm	A social norm, is a rule that is socially enforced. In social situations, such as meetings, they are unwritten and often unstated rules that govern individuals' behavior. A social norm is most evident when not followed or broken.
Norms	In testing, standards of test performance that permit the comparison of one person's score on

Go to **Cram101.com** for the Practice Tests for this Chapter.

Go to **Cram101.com** for the Practice Tests for this Chapter.
And, **NEVER** highlight a book again!

the test to the scores of others who have taken the same test are referred to as norms.

Right hemisphere	The brain is divided into left and right cerebral hemispheres. The right hemisphere of the cortex controls the left side of the body.
Motor cortex	Motor cortex refers to the section of cortex that lies in the frontal lobe, just across the central fissure from the sensory cortex. Neural impulses in the motor cortex are linked to muscular responses throughout the body.
Electrode	Any device used to electrically stimulate nerve tissue or to record its activity is an electrode.
Psychological test	Psychological test refers to a standardized measure of a sample of a person's behavior.
Rapid eye movement	Rapid eye movement is the stage of sleep during which the most vivid (though not all) dreams occur. During this stage, the eyes move rapidly, and the activity of the brain's neurons is quite similar to that during waking hours. It is the lightest form of sleep in that people awakened during REM usually feel alert and refreshed.
Rem sleep	Sleep characterized by rapid eye movements, paralysis of large muscles, fast and irregular heart rate and respiration rate, increased brain-wave activity, and vivid dreams is referred to as REM sleep. An infant spends about half the time in REM sleep when sleeping.
Lobes	The four major sections of the cerebral cortex: frontal, parietal, temporal, and occipital are called lobes.
Frontal lobe	The frontal lobe comprises four major folds of cortical tissue: the precentral gyrus, superior gyrus and the middle gyrus of the frontal gyri, the inferior frontal gyrus. It has been found to play a part in impulse control, judgement, language, memory, motor function, problem solving, sexual behavior, socialization and spontaneity.
Forebrain	The forebrain is the highest level of the brain. Key structures in the forebrain are the limbic system, thalamus, basal ganglia, hypothalamus, and cerebral cortex.
Stage theory	Stage theory characterizes development by hypothesizing the existence of distinct, and often critical, periods of life. Each period follows one another in an orderly sequence.
Psyche	Psyche is the soul, spirit, or mind as distinguished from the body. In psychoanalytic theory, it is the totality of the id, ego, and superego, including both conscious and unconscious components.
Melanie Klein	Melanie Klein built on the work of Sigmund Freud and was one of the theoretical cofounders of object relations theory. Her insistence on regarding aggression as an important force in its own right when analyzing children brought her into conflict with Anna Freud.
Anna Freud	Anna Freud was a pioneer of child psychoanalysis. She popularized the notion that adolescence is a period that includes rapid mood fluctuation with enormous uncertainty about self.
Nurture	Nurture refers to the environmental influences on behavior due to nutrition, culture, socioeconomic status, and learning.
Attitude	An enduring mental representation of a person, place, or thing that evokes an emotional response and related behavior is called attitude.
Bias	A bias is a prejudice in a general or specific sense, usually in the sense for having a preference to one particular point of view or ideological perspective.
Ideology	An ideology can be thought of as a comprehensive vision, as a way of looking at things, as in common sense and several philosophical tendencies, or a set of ideas proposed by the dominant class of a society to all members of this society.

Go to **Cram101.com** for the Practice Tests for this Chapter.

Go to **Cram101.com** for the Practice Tests for this Chapter.
And, **NEVER** highlight a book again!

Humanistic	Humanistic refers to any system of thought focused on subjective experience and human problems and potentials.
Determinism	Determinism is the philosophical proposition that every event, including human cognition and action, is causally determined by an unbroken chain of prior occurrences.
Illusion	An illusion is a distortion of a sensory perception.
Innate	Innate behavior is not learned or influenced by the environment, rather, it is present or predisposed at birth.
Teleology	While science investigates natural laws and phenomena, Philosophical naturalism and teleology investigate the existence or non-existence of an organizing principle behind those natural laws and phenonema. Philosophical naturalism asserts that there are no such principles. Teleology asserts that there are.
Causation	Causation concerns the time order relationship between two or more objects such that if a specific antecendent condition occurs the same consequent must always follow.
Motivation	In psychology, motivation is the driving force (desire) behind all actions of an organism.
Social influence	Social influence is when the actions or thoughts of individual(s) are changed by other individual(s). Peer pressure is an example of social influence.

Go to **Cram101.com** for the Practice Tests for this Chapter.

Sigmund Freud	Sigmund Freud was the founder of the psychoanalytic school, based on his theory that unconscious motives control much behavior, that particular kinds of unconscious thoughts and memories are the source of neurosis, and that neurosis could be treated through bringing these unconscious thoughts and memories to consciousness in psychoanalytic treatment.
Maslow	Maslow is mostly noted today for his proposal of a hierarchy of human needs which he often presented as a pyramid. Maslow was an instrumental player in the formation of the humanistic movement, also known as the third force in psychology.
Adler	Adler argued that human personality could be explained teleologically, separate strands dominated by the guiding purpose of the individual's unconscious self ideal to convert feelings of inferiority to superiority (or rather completeness). The desires of the self ideal were countered by social and ethical demands.
Consciousness	The awareness of the sensations, thoughts, and feelings being experienced at a given moment is called consciousness.
Infancy	The developmental period that extends from birth to 18 or 24 months is called infancy.
Guilt	Guilt describes many concepts related to a negative emotion or condition caused by actions which are believed to be, morally wrong. According to Freud, the avoidance of guilt is the basis for moral behavior.
Personality	Personality refers to the pattern of enduring characteristics that differentiates a person, the patterns of behaviors that make each individual unique.
Society	The social sciences use the term society to mean a group of people that form a semi-closed (or semi-open) social system, in which most interactions are with other individuals belonging to the group.
Psychoanalytic	Freud's theory that unconscious forces act as determinants of personality is called psychoanalytic theory. The theory is a developmental theory characterized by critical stages of development.
Individual psychology	Alfred Adler's individual psychology approach views people as motivated by purposes and goals, being creators of their own lives .
Attitude	An enduring mental representation of a person, place, or thing that evokes an emotional response and related behavior is called attitude.
Psychoanalysis	Psychoanalysis refers to the school of psychology that emphasizes the importance of unconscious motives and conflicts as determinants of human behavior. It was Freud's method of exploring human personality.
Theories	Theories are logically self-consistent models or frameworks describing the behavior of a certain natural or social phenomenon. They are broad explanations and predictions concerning phenomena of interest.
Psychodynamic	Most psychodynamic approaches are centered around the idea of a maladapted function developed early in life (usually childhood) which are at least in part unconscious. This maladapted function (a.k.a. defense mechanism) does not do well in place of a normal/healthy one.
Motivation	In psychology, motivation is the driving force (desire) behind all actions of an organism.
Compensation	In personaility, compensation, according to Adler, is an effort to overcome imagined or real inferiorities by developing one's abilities.
Infantile sexuality	Freud's insistence that sexuality does not begin with adolescence, that babies are sexual too, is referred to as infantile sexuality.
Drive for	The drive for superiority is Adler's term for the desire to compensate for feelings of

Go to **Cram101.com** for the Practice Tests for this Chapter.

superiority	inferiority.
Psychiatrist	A psychiatrist is a physician who specializes in the diagnosis and treatment of psychological disorders.
Rollo May	Rollo May was the best known American existential psychologist, authoring the influential book Love and Will in 1969. He differs from other humanistic psychologists in showing a sharper awareness of the tragic dimensions of human existence.
Sullivan	Sullivan developed the Self System, a configuration of the personality traits developed in childhood and reinforced by positive affirmation and the security operations developed in childhood to avoid anxiety and threats to self-esteem.
Rotter	Rotter focused on the application of social learning theory (SLT) to clinical psychology. She introduced the ideas of learning from generalized expectancies of reinforcement and internal/external locus of control (self-initiated change versus change influenced by others). According to Rotter, health outcomes could be improved by the development of a sense of personal control over one's life.
Karen Horney	Karen Horney, a neo-Freudian, deviated from orthodox Freudian analysis by emphasizing environmental and cultural, rather than biological, factors in neurosis.
Jung	Jung was in some aspects a response to Sigmund Freud's psychoanalysis. He proposed and developed the concepts of the extroverted and introverted personality, archetypes, and the collective unconscious. His work has been influential in psychiatry and in the study of religion, literature, and related fields.
Carl Rogers	Carl Rogers was instrumental in the development of non-directive psychotherapy, also known as "client-centered" psychotherapy. Rogers' basic tenets were unconditional positive regard, genuineness, and empathic understanding, with each demonstrated by the counselor.
Albert Ellis	Albert Ellis is a psychologist whose Rational Emotive Behavior Therapy (REBT), is the foundation of all cognitive and cognitive behavior therapies.
Insight	Insight refers to a sudden awareness of the relationships among various elements that had previously appeared to be independent of one another.
Perception	Perception is the process of acquiring, interpreting, selecting, and organizing sensory information.
Striving for superiority	According to Adler, the universal drive to adapt, improve oneself, and master life's challenges is referred to as striving for superiority.
Innate	Innate behavior is not learned or influenced by the environment, rather, it is present or predisposed at birth.
Analogy	An analogy is a comparison between two different things, in order to highlight some form of similarity. Analogy is the cognitive process of transferring information from a particular subject to another particular subject.
Shaping	The concept of reinforcing successive, increasingly accurate approximations to a target behavior is called shaping. The target behavior is broken down into a hierarchy of elemental steps, each step more sophisticated then the last. By successively reinforcing each of the the elemental steps, a form of differential reinforcement, until that step is learned while extinguishing the step below, the target behavior is gradually achieved.
Heredity	Heredity is the transfer of characteristics from parent to offspring through their genes.
Nurture	Nurture refers to the environmental influences on behavior due to nutrition, culture, socioeconomic status, and learning.

Go to **Cram101.com** for the Practice Tests for this Chapter.

Vaihinger	Vaihinger argued that human beings can never really know the underlying reality of the world, and that as a result we construct systems of thought and then assume that these match reality.
Free will	The idea that human beings are capable of freely making choices or decisions is free will.
Teleology	While science investigates natural laws and phenomena, Philosophical naturalism and teleology investigate the existence or non-existence of an organizing principle behind those natural laws and phenemena. Philosophical naturalism asserts that there are no such principles. Teleology asserts that there are.
Causation	Causation concerns the time order relationship between two or more objects such that if a specific antecedent condition occurs the same consequent must always follow.
Affect	A subjective feeling or emotional tone often accompanied by bodily expressions noticeable to others is called affect.
Unconscious thought	Unconscious thought is Freud's concept of a reservoir of unacceptable wishes, feelings, and thoughts that are beyond conscious awareness.
Empathy	Empathy is the recognition and understanding of the states of mind, including beliefs, desires and particularly emotions of others without injecting your own.
Species	Species refers to a reproductively isolated breeding population.
Senses	The senses are systems that consist of a sensory cell type that respond to a specific kind of physical energy, and that correspond to a defined region within the brain where the signals are received and interpreted.
Attachment	Attachment is the tendency to seek closeness to another person and feel secure when that person is present.
Identical twins	Identical twins occur when a single egg is fertilized to form one zygote (monozygotic) but the zygote then divides into two separate embryos. The two embryos develop into foetuses sharing the same womb. Monozygotic twins are genetically identical unless there has been a mutation in development, and they are almost always the same gender.
Maladjustment	Maladjustment is the condition of being unable to adapt properly to your environment with resulting emotional instability.
Congenital	A condition existing at birth is referred to as congenital.
Anxiety	Anxiety is a complex combination of the feeling of fear, apprehension and worry often accompanied by physical sensations such as palpitations, chest pain and/or shortness of breath.
Ego	In Freud's view the Ego serves to balance our primitive needs and our moral beliefs and taboos. Relying on experience, a healthy Ego provides the ability to adapt to reality and interact with the outside world.
Suicide	Suicide behavior is rare in childhood but escalates in adolescence. The suicide rate increases in a linear fashion from adolescence through late adulthood.
Masochism	The counterpart of sadism is masochism, the sexual pleasure or gratification of having pain or suffering inflicted upon the self, often consisting of sexual fantasies or urges for being beaten, humiliated, bound, tortured, or otherwise made to suffer, either as an enhancement to or a substitute for sexual pleasure.
Depression	In everyday language depression refers to any downturn in mood, which may be relatively transitory and perhaps due to something trivial. This is differentiated from Clinical depression which is marked by symptoms that last two weeks or more and are so severe that

they interfere with daily living.

Regression	Return to a form of behavior characteristic of an earlier stage of development is called regression.
Anatomy	Anatomy is the branch of biology that deals with the structure and organization of living things. It can be divided into animal anatomy (zootomy) and plant anatomy (phytonomy). Major branches of anatomy include comparative anatomy, histology, and human anatomy.
Psychotherapy	Psychotherapy is a set of techniques based on psychological principles intended to improve mental health, emotional or behavioral issues. Commonly psychotherapy involves a therapist and client(s), who discuss their issues in an effort to discover what they are and how they can solve them.
Postulates	Postulates are general statements about behavior that cannot be directly verified. They are used to generate theorems which can be tested.
Psychopathology	Psychopathology refers to the field concerned with the nature and development of mental disorders.
Trait	An enduring personality characteristic that tends to lead to certain behaviors is called a trait. The term trait also means a genetically inherited feature of an organism.
Reliability	Reliability means the extent to which a test produces a consistent , reproducible score .
Personality trait	According to the Diagnostic and Statistical Manual of the American Psychiatric Association, a personality trait is a "prominent aspect of personality that is exhibited in a wide range of important social and personal contexts. ...".
Interrater reliability	Interrater reliability is the correlation between ratings of two or more raters in a given research study.
Openness to Experience	Openness to Experience, one of the big-five traits, describes a dimension of cognitive style that distinguishes imaginative, creative people from down-to-earth, conventional people.
Neuroticism	Eysenck's use of the term neuroticism (or Emotional Stability) was proposed as the dimension describing individual differences in the predisposition towards neurotic disorder.
Extraversion	Extraversion, one of the big-five personailty traits, is marked by pronounced engagement with the external world. They are people who enjoy being with people, are full of energy, and often experience positive emotions.
Conscientiou-ness	Conscientiousness is one of the dimensions of the five-factor model of personality and individual differences involving being organized, thorough, and reliable as opposed to careless, negligent, and unreliable.
Agreeableness	Agreeableness, one of the big-five personality traits, reflects individual differences in concern with cooperation and social harmony. It is the degree individuals value getting along with others.
Creativity	Creativity is the ability to think about something in novel and unusual ways and come up with unique solutions to problems. It involves divergent thinking, having many solutions or views to a problem.
Early childhood	Early childhood refers to the developmental period extending from the end of infancy to about 5 or 6 years of age; sometimes called the preschool years.
Variable	A variable refers to a measurable factor, characteristic, or attribute of an individual or a system.
Construct	A generalized concept, such as anxiety or gravity, is a construct.

Go to **Cram101.com** for the Practice Tests for this Chapter.

Operational definition	An operational definition is the definition of a concept or action in terms of the observable and repeatable process, procedures, and appartaus that illustrates the concept or action.
Parsimony	In science, parsimony is preference for the least complicated explanation for an observation. This is generally regarded as good when judging hypotheses. Occam's Razor also states the "principle of parsimony".
Free choice	Free choice refers to the ability to freely make choices that are not controlled by genetics, learning, or unconscious forces.

Teleology	While science investigates natural laws and phenomena, Philosophical naturalism and teleology investigate the existence or non-existence of an organizing principle behind those natural laws and phenomena. Philosophical naturalism asserts that there are no such principles. Teleology asserts that there are.
Regression	Return to a form of behavior characteristic of an earlier stage of development is called regression.
Theories	Theories are logically self-consistent models or frameworks describing the behavior of a certain natural or social phenomenon. They are broad explanations and predictions concerning phenomena of interest.
Stages	Stages represent relatively discrete periods of time in which functioning is qualitatively different from functioning at other periods.
Persona	In Jungian archetypal psychology, the Persona is the mask or appearance one presents to the world. It may appear in dreams under various guises.
Personal unconscious	The personal unconscious in Jung's theory is the layer of the unconscious containing all of the thoughts and experiences that are accessible to the conscious, as well as the repressed memories and impulses.
Personality	Personality refers to the pattern of enduring characteristics that differentiates a person, the patterns of behaviors that make each individual unique.
Personality type	A persistent style of complex behaviors defined by a group of related traits is referred to as a personality type. Myer Friedman and his co-workers first defined personality types in the 1950s. Friedman classified people into 2 categories, Type A and Type B.
Psyche	Psyche is the soul, spirit, or mind as distinguished from the body. In psychoanalytic theory, it is the totality of the id, ego, and superego, including both conscious and unconscious components.
Psychodynamic	Most psychodynamic approaches are centered around the idea of a maladapted function developed early in life (usually childhood) which are at least in part unconscious. This maladapted function (a.k.a. defense mechanism) does not do well in place of a normal/healthy one.
Psychotherapy	Psychotherapy is a set of techniques based on psychological principles intended to improve mental health, emotional or behavioral issues. Commonly psychotherapy involves a therapist and client(s), who discuss their issues in an effort to discover what they are and how they can solve them.
Introversion	A personality trait characterized by intense imagination and a tendency to inhibit impulses is called introversion.
Jung	Jung was in some aspects a response to Sigmund Freud's psychoanalysis. He proposed and developed the concepts of the extroverted and introverted personality, archetypes, and the collective unconscious. His work has been influential in psychiatry and in the study of religion, literature, and related fields.
Dream analysis	Dream analysis is a part of psychoanalysis that intends to look beneath the manifest content of a dream, i.e., what we perceive in the dream, to the latent content of a dream, i.e., the meaning of the dream and the reason we dreamt it.
Extraversion	Extraversion, one of the big-five personailty traits, is marked by pronounced engagement with the external world. They are people who enjoy being with people, are full of energy, and often experience positive emotions.
Attitude	An enduring mental representation of a person, place, or thing that evokes an emotional response and related behavior is called attitude.

Go to **Cram101.com** for the Practice Tests for this Chapter.

Causation	Causation concerns the time order relationship between two or more objects such that if a specific antecedent condition occurs the same consequent must always follow.
Collective unconscious	Collective unconscious is a term of analytical psychology, originally coined by Carl Jung. It refers to that part of a person's unconscious which is common to all human beings. It contains archetypes, which are forms or symbols that are manifested by all people in all cultures.
Analytical psychology	Analytical psychology is based upon the movement started by Carl Jung and his followers as distinct from Freudian psychoanalysis. Its aim is the personal experience of the deep forces and motivations underlying human behavior.
Anima	Anima, according to Carl Jung, is the feminine side of a man's personal unconscious. It can be identified as all the unconscious feminine psychological qualities that a man possesses.
Archetype	The archetype is a concept of psychologist Carl Jung. They are innate prototypes for ideas, which may subsequently become involved in the interpretation of observed phenomena. A group of memories and interpretations closely associated with an archetype is called a complex.
Sigmund Freud	Sigmund Freud was the founder of the psychoanalytic school, based on his theory that unconscious motives control much behavior, that particular kinds of unconscious thoughts and memories are the source of neurosis, and that neurosis could be treated through bringing these unconscious thoughts and memories to consciousness in psychoanalytic treatment.
Goethe	Goethe argued that laws could not be created by pure rationalism, since geography and history shaped habits and patterns. This stood in sharp contrast to the prevailing Enlightenment view that reason was sufficient to create well-ordered societies and good laws.
Adolescence	The period of life bounded by puberty and the assumption of adult responsibilities is adolescence.
Reflection	Reflection is the process of rephrasing or repeating thoughts and feelings expressed, making the person more aware of what they are saying or thinking.
Intuition	Quick, impulsive thought that does not make use of formal logic or clear reasoning is referred to as intuition.
Ego	In Freud's view the Ego serves to balance our primitive needs and our moral beliefs and taboos. Relying on experience, a healthy Ego provides the ability to adapt to reality and interact with the outside world.
Bleuler	Bleuler is particularly notable for naming schizophrenia, a disorder which was previously known as dementia praecox. Bleuler realised the condition was neither a dementia, nor did it always occur in young people (praecox meaning early) and so gave the condition the name from the Greek for split (schizo) and mind (phrene).
Charcot	Charcot took an interest in the malady then called hysteria. It seemed to be a mental disorder with physical manifestations, of immediate interest to a neurologist. He believed that hysteria was the result of a weak neurological system which was hereditary.
Stanley Hall	His laboratory at Johns Hopkins is considered to be the first American laboratory of psychology. In 1887 Stanley Hall founded the American Journal of Psychology. His interests centered around child development and evolutionary theory
Psychoanalyst	A psychoanalyst is a specially trained therapist who attempts to treat the individual by uncovering and revealing to the individual otherwise subconscious factors that are contributing to some undesirable behavor.
Consciousness	The awareness of the sensations, thoughts, and feelings being experienced at a given moment is called consciousness.

Go to **Cram101.com** for the Practice Tests for this Chapter.

Threshold	In general, a threshold is a fixed location or value where an abrupt change is observed. In the sensory modalities, it is the minimum amount of stimulus energy necessary to elicit a sensory response.
Preconscious	In psychodynamic theory, material that is not in awareness but that can be brought into awareness by focusing one's attention is referred to as preconscious.
Emotion	An emotion is a mental states that arise spontaneously, rather than through conscious effort. They are often accompanied by physiological changes.
Innate	Innate behavior is not learned or influenced by the environment, rather, it is present or predisposed at birth.
Predisposition	Predisposition refers to an inclination or diathesis to respond in a certain way, either inborn or acquired. In abnormal psychology, it is a factor that lowers the ability to withstand stress and inclines the individual toward pathology.
Perception	Perception is the process of acquiring, interpreting, selecting, and organizing sensory information.
Instinct	Instinct is the word used to describe inherent dispositions towards particular actions. They are generally an inherited pattern of responses or reactions to certain kinds of situations.
Introspection	Introspection is the self report or consideration of one's own thoughts, perceptions and mental processes. Classic introspection was done through trained observers.
Delusion	A false belief, not generally shared by others, and that cannot be changed despite strong evidence to the contrary is a delusion.
Paranoid	The term paranoid is typically used in a general sense to signify any self-referential delusion, or more specifically, to signify a delusion involving the fear of persecution.
Hallucination	A hallucination is a sensory perception experienced in the absence of an external stimulus, as distinct from an illusion, which is a misperception of an external stimulus. They may occur in any sensory modality - visual, auditory, olfactory, gustatory, tactile, or mixed.
Psychiatrist	A psychiatrist is a physician who specializes in the diagnosis and treatment of psychological disorders.
Oedipus complex	The Oedipus complex is a concept developed by Sigmund Freud to explain the maturation of the infant boy through identification with the father and desire for the mother.
Accommodation	Piaget's developmental process of accommodation is the modification of currently held schemes or new schemes so that new information inconsistent with the existing schemes can be integrated and understood.
Society	The social sciences use the term society to mean a group of people that form a semi-closed (or semi-open) social system, in which most interactions are with other individuals belonging to the group.
Individuality	According to Cooper, individuality consists of two dimensions: self-assertion and separateness.
Repression	A defense mechanism, repression involves moving thoughts unacceptable to the ego into the unconscious, where they cannot be easily accessed.
Projection	Attributing one's own undesirable thoughts, impulses, traits, or behaviors to others is referred to as projection.
Learning	Learning is a relatively permanent change in behavior that results from experience. Thus, to attribute a behavioral change to learning, the change must be relatively permanent and must result from experience.

Go to **Cram101.com** for the Practice Tests for this Chapter.

Visual perception	Visual perception is one of the senses, consisting of the ability to detect light and interpret it. Vision has a specific sensory system.
Wisdom	Wisdom is the ability to make correct judgments and decisions. It is an intangible quality gained through experience. Whether or not something is wise is determined in a pragmatic sense by its popularity, how long it has been around, and its ability to predict against future events.
Femininity	Femininity is the set of characteristics defined by a culture for idealized females.
Midlife crisis	Midlife crisis refers to a period of turmoil usually occurring in a person's 40s and brought on by an awareness of one's mortality; characterized by a reassessment of one's life and a decision to make changes, either drastic or moderate, in order to make the remaining years better.
Autonomy	Autonomy is the condition of something that does not depend on anything else.
Motivation	In psychology, motivation is the driving force (desire) behind all actions of an organism.
Early childhood	Early childhood refers to the developmental period extending from the end of infancy to about 5 or 6 years of age; sometimes called the preschool years.
Adler	Adler argued that human personality could be explained teleologically, separate strands dominated by the guiding purpose of the individual's unconscious self ideal to convert feelings of inferiority to superiority (or rather completeness). The desires of the self ideal were countered by social and ethical demands.
Adaptation	Adaptation is a lowering of sensitivity to a stimulus following prolonged exposure to that stimulus. Behavioral adaptations are special ways a particular organism behaves to survive in its natural habitat.
Introvert	Introvert refers to a person whose attention is focused inward; a shy, reserved, timid person.
Bias	A bias is a prejudice in a general or specific sense, usually in the sense for having a preference to one particular point of view or ideological perspective.
Pragmatism	Pragmatism is characterized by the insistence on consequences, utility and practicality as vital components of truth. Pragmatism objects to the view that human concepts and intellect represent reality, and therefore stands in opposition to both formalist and rationalist schools of philosophy.
Creativity	Creativity is the ability to think about something in novel and unusual ways and come up with unique solutions to problems. It involves divergent thinking, having many solutions or views to a problem.
Physiological changes	Alterations in heart rate, blood pressure, perspiration, and other involuntary responses are physiological changes.
Stimulus	A change in an environmental condition that elicits a response is a stimulus.
Sensation	Sensation is the first stage in the chain of biochemical and neurologic events that begins with the impinging of a stimulus upon the receptor cells of a sensory organ, which then leads to perception, the mental state that is reflected in statements like "I see a uniformly blue wall."
Motives	Needs or desires that energize and direct behavior toward a goal are motives.
Puberty	Puberty refers to the process of physical changes by which a child's body becomes an adult body capable of reproduction.
Anxiety	Anxiety is a complex combination of the feeling of fear, apprehension and worry often

accompanied by physical sensations such as palpitations, chest pain and/or shortness of breath.

Physical attractiveness	Physical attractiveness is the perception of an individual as physically beautiful by other people.
Illusion	An illusion is a distortion of a sensory perception.
Homogeneous	In biology homogeneous has a meaning similar to its meaning in mathematics. Generally it means "the same" or "of the same quality or general property".
Validity	The extent to which a test measures what it is intended to measure is called validity.
Hypothesis	A specific statement about behavior or mental processes that is testable through research is a hypothesis.
Galvanic skin response	Galvanic skin response is a method of measuring the electrical resistance of the skin and interpreting it as an image of activity in certain parts of the body.
Memory trace	A memory trace is the postulated assumed change in the nervous system that reflects the impression made by a stimulus. They are said to be held in sensory registers.
Penis	The penis is the external male copulatory organ and the external male organ of urination. In humans, the penis is homologous to the female clitoris, as it develops from the same embryonic structure. It is capable of erection for use in copulation.
Species	Species refers to a reproductively isolated breeding population.
Transference	Transference is a phenomenon in psychology characterized by unconscious redirection of feelings from one person to another.
Countertrans-erence	Feelings that the psychoanalyst unconsciously directs to the analysis, stemming from his or her own emotional vulnerabilities and unresolved conflicts are countertransference effects.
Acute	Acute means sudden, sharp, and abrupt. Usually short in duration.
Hume	Hume was the ultimate skeptic, reducing matter, mind, religion, and science to a matter of sense impressions and memories. He was a strong empiricist.
Population	Population refers to all members of a well-defined group of organisms, events, or things.
Norms	In testing, standards of test performance that permit the comparison of one person's score on the test to the scores of others who have taken the same test are referred to as norms.
Descriptive research	Descriptive research is also known as statistical research. It describes data about the population being studied. Descriptive reseach answers the following questions: who, what, where, when and how.
Clinician	A health professional authorized to provide services to people suffering from one or more pathologies is a clinician.
Trauma	Trauma refers to a severe physical injury or wound to the body caused by an external force, or a psychological shock having a lasting effect on mental life.
Empirical	Empirical means the use of working hypotheses which are capable of being disproved using observation or experiment.
Operational definition	An operational definition is the definition of a concept or action in terms of the observable and repeatable process, procedures, and appartaus that illustrates the concept or action.
Parsimony	In science, parsimony is preference for the least complicated explanation for an observation. This is generally regarded as good when judging hypotheses. Occam's Razor also states the "principle of parsimony".

Law of parsimony	The law of parsimony states that entities should not be multiplied needlessly; the simplest of two competing theories is to be preferred.
Limited capacity	Limited capacity refers to the concept that one's information processing ability is restricted. Metaphors for capacity include mental space, mental energy or effort, and time.
Prejudice	Prejudice in general, implies coming to a judgment on the subject before learning where the preponderance of the evidence actually lies, or formation of a judgement without direct experience.

Society	The social sciences use the term society to mean a group of people that form a semi-closed (or semi-open) social system, in which most interactions are with other individuals belonging to the group.
Melanie Klein	Melanie Klein built on the work of Sigmund Freud and was one of the theoretical cofounders of object relations theory. Her insistence on regarding aggression as an important force in its own right when analyzing children brought her into conflict with Anna Freud.
Anna Freud	Anna Freud was a pioneer of child psychoanalysis. She popularized the notion that adolescence is a period that includes rapid mood fluctuation with enormous uncertainty about self.
Object relation	Object relation theory is the idea that the ego-self exists only in relation to other objects, which may be external or internal.
Object relations theory	Object relations theory holds that the ego-self exists only in relation to other objects, which may be external or internal. The internal objects are internalized versions of external objects, primarily formed from early interactions with the parents.
Prototype	A concept of a category of objects or events that serves as a good example of the category is called a prototype.
Affect	A subjective feeling or emotional tone often accompanied by bodily expressions noticeable to others is called affect.
Theories	Theories are logically self-consistent models or frameworks describing the behavior of a certain natural or social phenomenon. They are broad explanations and predictions concerning phenomena of interest.
Psychodynamic	Most psychodynamic approaches are centered around the idea of a maladapted function developed early in life (usually childhood) which are at least in part unconscious. This maladapted function (a.k.a. defense mechanism) does not do well in place of a normal/healthy one.
Kohut	Kohut was a pioneer in the fields of psychology and psychiatry. He established the school of Self Psychology as a branch of psychoanalysis. Where Freud emphasized guilt in the etiology of emotional disorders, Kohut saw shame as more central.
Infancy	The developmental period that extends from birth to 18 or 24 months is called infancy.
Bowlby	Bowlby, a developmental psychologist of the psychoanalytic tradition, was responsible for much of the early research conducted on attachment in humans. He identified three stages of separation: protest, despair, and detachment.
Attachment	Attachment is the tendency to seek closeness to another person and feel secure when that person is present.
Attachment style	Attachment style refers to the way a person typically interacts with significant others.
Psychoanalysis	Psychoanalysis refers to the school of psychology that emphasizes the importance of unconscious motives and conflicts as determinants of human behavior. It was Freud's method of exploring human personality.
Psychoanalyst	A psychoanalyst is a specially trained therapist who attempts to treat the individual by uncovering and revealing to the individual otherwise subconscious factors that are contributing to some undesirable behavor.
Karen Horney	Karen Horney, a neo-Freudian, deviated from orthodox Freudian analysis by emphasizing environmental and cultural, rather than biological, factors in neurosis.
Psychoanalytic	Freud's theory that unconscious forces act as determinants of personality is called psychoanalytic theory. The theory is a developmental theory characterized by critical stages of development.

Go to **Cram101.com** for the Practice Tests for this Chapter.

Go to **Cram101.com** for the Practice Tests for this Chapter.
And, **NEVER** highlight a book again!

Child development	Scientific study of the processes of change from conception through adolescence is called child development.
Case study	A carefully drawn biography that may be obtained through interviews, questionnaires, and psychological tests is called a case study.
Superego	Frued's third psychic structure, which functions as a moral guardian and sets forth high standards for behavior is the superego.
Psychoanalytic theory	Psychoanalytic theory is a general term for approaches to psychoanalysis which attempt to provide a conceptual framework more-or-less independent of clinical practice rather than based on empirical analysis of clinical cases.
Early childhood	Early childhood refers to the developmental period extending from the end of infancy to about 5 or 6 years of age; sometimes called the preschool years.
Suicide	Suicide behavior is rare in childhood but escalates in adolescence. The suicide rate increases in a linear fashion from adolescence through late adulthood.
Instinct	Instinct is the word used to describe inherent dispositions towards particular actions. They are generally an inherited pattern of responses or reactions to certain kinds of situations.
Instinct theory	The notion that human behavior is motivated by certain innate tendencies, or instincts, shared by all individuals is an instinct theory.
Separation anxiety	Separation anxiety is a psychological condition in which an individual has excessive anxiety regarding separation from home, or from those with whom the individual has a strong attachment.
Stages	Stages represent relatively discrete periods of time in which functioning is qualitatively different from functioning at other periods.
Autonomy	Autonomy is the condition of something that does not depend on anything else.
Anxiety	Anxiety is a complex combination of the feeling of fear, apprehension and worry often accompanied by physical sensations such as palpitations, chest pain and/or shortness of breath.
Penis	The penis is the external male copulatory organ and the external male organ of urination. In humans, the penis is homologous to the female clitoris, as it develops from the same embryonic structure. It is capable of erection for use in copulation.
Predisposition	Predisposition refers to an inclination or diathesis to respond in a certain way, either inborn or acquired. In abnormal psychology, it is a factor that lowers the ability to withstand stress and inclines the individual toward pathology.
Death instinct	The death instinct was defined by Sigmund Freud, in Beyond the Pleasure Principle(1920). It speculated on the existence of a fundamental death wish or death instinct, referring to an individual's own need to die.
Innate	Innate behavior is not learned or influenced by the environment, rather, it is present or predisposed at birth.
Oedipus complex	The Oedipus complex is a concept developed by Sigmund Freud to explain the maturation of the infant boy through identification with the father and desire for the mother.
Creativity	Creativity is the ability to think about something in novel and unusual ways and come up with unique solutions to problems. It involves divergent thinking, having many solutions or views to a problem.
Sensation	Sensation is the first stage in the chain of biochemical and neurologic events that begins with the impinging of a stimulus upon the receptor cells of a sensory organ, which then leads

Go to **Cram101.com** for the Practice Tests for this Chapter.

to perception, the mental state that is reflected in statements like "I see a uniformly blue wall."

Ego

In Freud's view the Ego serves to balance our primitive needs and our moral beliefs and taboos. Relying on experience, a healthy Ego provides the ability to adapt to reality and interact with the outside world.

Dichotomy

A dichotomy is the division of a proposition into two parts which are both mutually exclusive – i.e. both cannot be simultaneously true – and jointly exhaustive – i.e. they cover the full range of possible outcomes. They are often contrasting and spoken of as "opposites".

Paranoid

The term paranoid is typically used in a general sense to signify any self-referential delusion, or more specifically, to signify a delusion involving the fear of persecution.

Perception

Perception is the process of acquiring, interpreting, selecting, and organizing sensory information.

Guilt

Guilt describes many concepts related to a negative emotion or condition caused by actions which are believed to be, morally wrong. According to Freud, the avoidance of guilt is the basis for moral behavior.

Ambivalence

The simultaneous holding of strong positive and negative emotional attitudes toward the same situation or person is called ambivalence.

Empathy

Empathy is the recognition and understanding of the states of mind, including beliefs, desires and particularly emotions of others without injecting your own.

Projection

Attributing one's own undesirable thoughts, impulses, traits, or behaviors to others is referred to as projection.

Introjection

Introjection is a psychological process where the subject replicates in itself behaviors, attributes or other fragments of the surrounding world, especially of other subjects. Cognate concepts are identification, incorporation and internalization.

Internalization

The developmental change from behavior that is externally controlled to behavior that is controlled by internal standards and principles is referred to as internalization.

Libido

Sigmund Freud suggested that libido is the instinctual energy or force that can come into conflict with the conventions of civilized behavior. Jung, condidered the libido as the free creative, or psychic, energy an individual has to put toward personal development, or individuation.

Phallic stage

The phallic stage is the 3rd of Freud's psychosexual stages, when awareness of and manipulation of the genitals is supposed to be a primary source of pleasure. In this stage the child deals with the Oedipus complex, if male, or the Electra Complex, if female.

Anal stage

The anal stage in psychology is the term used by Sigmund Freud to describe the development during the second year of life, in which a child's pleasure and conflict centers are in the anal area.

Attitude

An enduring mental representation of a person, place, or thing that evokes an emotional response and related behavior is called attitude.

Positive relationship

Statistically, a positive relationship refers to a mathematical relationship in which increases in one measure are matched by increases in the other.

Homosexual

Homosexual refers to a sexual orientation characterized by aesthetic attraction, romantic love, and sexual desire exclusively for members of the same sex or gender identity.

Castration

Castration is any action, surgical, chemical or otherwise, by which a biological male loses use of the testes. This causes sterilization, i.e. prevents him from reproducing; it also

Go to **Cram101.com** for the Practice Tests for this Chapter.

	greatly reduces the production of certain hormones, such as testosterone.
Castration anxiety	Castration anxiety is a fear posited by Sigmund Freud in his writings on the Oedipus complex at the genital stage of sexual development. It asserts that boys seeing a girl's genitalia will falsely assume that the girl must have had her penis removed, probably as punishment for some misbehavior, and will be anxious lest the same happen to him.
Crucial stage	Third of four of Jellinek's stages identified in the progression of alcoholism, is the crucial stage involving a loss of control of drinking and occasional binges of heavy drinking.
Postnatal	Postnatal is the period beginning immediately after the birth of a child and extending for about six weeks. The period is also known as postpartum and, less commonly, puerperium.
Primary caregiver	Primary caregiver refers to a person primarily responsible for the care of an infant, usually the infant's mother or father.
Autism	Autism is a neurodevelopmental disorder that manifests itself in markedly abnormal social interaction, communication ability, patterns of interests, and patterns of behavior.
Analogy	An analogy is a comparison between two different things, in order to highlight some form of similarity. Analogy is the cognitive process of transferring information from a particular subject to another particular subject.
Personal identity	The portion of the self-concept that pertains to the self as a distinct, separate individual is called personal identity.
Delusion	A false belief, not generally shared by others, and that cannot be changed despite strong evidence to the contrary is a delusion.
Acquisition	Acquisition is the process of adapting to the environment, learning or becoming conditioned. In classical conditoning terms, it is the initial learning of the stimulus response link, which involves a neutral stimulus being associated with a unconditioned stimulus and becoming a conditioned stimulus.
Individuality	According to Cooper, individuality consists of two dimensions: self-assertion and separateness.
Empirical	Empirical means the use of working hypotheses which are capable of being disproved using observation or experiment.
Inference	Inference is the act or process of drawing a conclusion based solely on what one already knows.
Regression	Return to a form of behavior characteristic of an earlier stage of development is called regression.
Neurologist	A physician who studies the nervous system, especially its structure, functions, and abnormalities is referred to as neurologist.
Personality	Personality refers to the pattern of enduring characteristics that differentiates a person, the patterns of behaviors that make each individual unique.
Shaping	The concept of reinforcing successive, increasingly accurate approximations to a target behavior is called shaping. The target behavior is broken down into a hierarchy of elemental steps, each step more sophisticated then the last. By successively reinforcing each of the the elemental steps, a form of differential reinforcement, until that step is learned while extinguishing the step below, the target behavior is gradually achieved.
Psychotherapy	Psychotherapy is a set of techniques based on psychological principles intended to improve mental health, emotional or behavioral issues. Commonly psychotherapy involves a therapist

Go to **Cram101.com** for the Practice Tests for this Chapter.

and client(s), who discuss their issues in an effort to discover what they are and how they can solve them.

Attachment theory	Attachment theory is a theory about the psychological tendency to seek closeness to another person and feel secure when that person is present. A criticism of the theory is that it ignores the diversity of socializing agents and contexts that exists.
Psychiatrist	A psychiatrist is a physician who specializes in the diagnosis and treatment of psychological disorders.
Motivation	In psychology, motivation is the driving force (desire) behind all actions of an organism.
Empiricism	Empiricism is generally regarded as being at the heart of the modern scientific method, that our theories should be based on our observations of the world rather than on intuition, or deductive logic.
Ethology	Where comparative psychology sees the study of animal behavior in the context of what is known about human psychology, ethology sees the study of animal behavior in the context of what is known about animal anatomy and physiology.
Evolutionary perspective	A perspective that focuses on how humans have evolved and adapted behaviors required for survival against various environmental pressures over the long course is called the evolutionary perspective.
Evolutionary theory	Evolutionary theory is concerned with heritable variability rather than behavioral variations. Natural selection requirements: (1) natural variability within a species must exist, (2) only some individual differences are heritable, and (3) natural selection only takes place when there is an interaction between the inborn attributes of organisms and the environment in which they live.
Emotion	An emotion is a mental states that arise spontaneously, rather than through conscious effort. They are often accompanied by physiological changes.
Friendship	The essentials of friendship are reciprocity and commitment between individuals who see themselves more or less as equals. Interaction between friends rests on a more equal power base than the interaction between children and adults.
Trait	An enduring personality characteristic that tends to lead to certain behaviors is called a trait. The term trait also means a genetically inherited feature of an organism.
Strange situation	An observational measure of infant attachment that requires the infant to move through a series of introductions, separations, and reunions with the caregiver and an adult stranger in a prescribed order is called Ainsworth's strange situation.
Insecure attachment	Insecure attachment occurs when infants either avoid the caregiver or show considerable resistance or ambivalence toward the caregiver.
Transference	Transference is a phenomenon in psychology characterized by unconscious redirection of feelings from one person to another.
Motives	Needs or desires that energize and direct behavior toward a goal are motives.
Eating disorders	Psychological disorders characterized by distortion of the body image and gross disturbances in eating patterns are called eating disorders.
Graham	Graham has conducted a number of studies that reveal stronger socioeconomic-status influences rather than ethnic influences in achievement.
Egocentricity	Egocentricity in Piaget's theory is the tendency to interpret objects and events from one's own perspective.
Gender	A gender difference is a disparity between genders involving quality or quantity. Though some

Go to **Cram101.com** for the Practice Tests for this Chapter.

difference	gender differences are controversial, they are not to be confused with sexist stereotypes.
Egocentrism	The inability to distinguish between one's own perspective and someone else's is referred to as egocentrism.
Questionnaire	A self-report method of data collection or clinical assessment method in which the individual being studied checks off items on a printed list, answers multiple-choice questions, or writes out answers to essay questions aimed at producing a selfdescription is called questionnaire.
Parental responsiveness	Parental responsiveness is the degree of caregiving that is based on sensitivity to a child's feelings, needs, rhythms, and signals.
Psyche	Psyche is the soul, spirit, or mind as distinguished from the body. In psychoanalytic theory, it is the totality of the id, ego, and superego, including both conscious and unconscious components.
Parsimony	In science, parsimony is preference for the least complicated explanation for an observation. This is generally regarded as good when judging hypotheses. Occam's Razor also states the "principle of parsimony".
Free choice	Free choice refers to the ability to freely make choices that are not controlled by genetics, learning, or unconscious forces.
Determinism	Determinism is the philosophical proposition that every event, including human cognition and action, is causally determined by an unbroken chain of prior occurrences.
Teleology	While science investigates natural laws and phenomena, Philosophical naturalism and teleology investigate the existence or non-existence of an organizing principle behind those natural laws and phenonema. Philosophical naturalism asserts that there are no such principles. Teleology asserts that there are.
Causation	Causation concerns the time order relationship between two or more objects such that if a specific antecendent condition occurs the same consequent must always follow.
Clinician	A health professional authorized to provide services to people suffering from one or more pathologies is a clinician.
Punishment	Punishment is the addtion of a stimulus that reduces the frequency of a response, or the removal of a stimulus that results in a reduction of the response.

Shaping	The concept of reinforcing successive, increasingly accurate approximations to a target behavior is called shaping. The target behavior is broken down into a hierarchy of elemental steps, each step more sophisticated then the last. By successively reinforcing each of the the elemental steps, a form of differential reinforcement, until that step is learned while extinguishing the step below, the target behavior is gradually achieved.
Personality	Personality refers to the pattern of enduring characteristics that differentiates a person, the patterns of behaviors that make each individual unique.
Psychoanalytic	Freud's theory that unconscious forces act as determinants of personality is called psychoanalytic theory. The theory is a developmental theory characterized by critical stages of development.
Karen Horney	Karen Horney, a neo-Freudian, deviated from orthodox Freudian analysis by emphasizing environmental and cultural, rather than biological, factors in neurosis.
Basic anxiety	Basic anxiety is a child's insecurity and doubt when a parent is indifferent, unloving, or disparaging. This anxiety, according to Horney, leads the child to a basic hostility toward his or her parents. The child may then become neurotic as an adult.
Anxiety	Anxiety is a complex combination of the feeling of fear, apprehension and worry often accompanied by physical sensations such as palpitations, chest pain and/or shortness of breath.
Reflection	Reflection is the process of rephrasing or repeating thoughts and feelings expressed, making the person more aware of what they are saying or thinking.
Insight	Insight refers to a sudden awareness of the relationships among various elements that had previously appeared to be independent of one another.
Theories	Theories are logically self-consistent models or frameworks describing the behavior of a certain natural or social phenomenon. They are broad explanations and predictions concerning phenomena of interest.
Psychodynamic	Most psychodynamic approaches are centered around the idea of a maladapted function developed early in life (usually childhood) which are at least in part unconscious. This maladapted function (a.k.a. defense mechanism) does not do well in place of a normal/healthy one.
Melanie Klein	Melanie Klein built on the work of Sigmund Freud and was one of the theoretical cofounders of object relations theory. Her insistence on regarding aggression as an important force in its own right when analyzing children brought her into conflict with Anna Freud.
Psychoanalysis	Psychoanalysis refers to the school of psychology that emphasizes the importance of unconscious motives and conflicts as determinants of human behavior. It was Freud's method of exploring human personality.
Psychoanalyst	A psychoanalyst is a specially trained therapist who attempts to treat the individual by uncovering and revealing to the individual otherwise subconscious factors that are contributing to some undesirable behavior.
Sullivan	Sullivan developed the Self System, a configuration of the personality traits developed in childhood and reinforced by positive affirmation and the security operations developed in childhood to avoid anxiety and threats to self-esteem.
Neurosis	Neurosis, any mental disorder that, although may cause distress, does not interfere with rational thought or the persons' ability to function.
Jung	Jung was in some aspects a response to Sigmund Freud's psychoanalysis. He proposed and developed the concepts of the extroverted and introverted personality, archetypes, and the collective unconscious. His work has been influential in psychiatry and in the study of

Go to **Cram101.com** for the Practice Tests for this Chapter.

	religion, literature, and related fields.
Adler	Adler argued that human personality could be explained teleologically, separate strands dominated by the guiding purpose of the individual's unconscious self ideal to convert feelings of inferiority to superiority (or rather completeness). The desires of the self ideal were countered by social and ethical demands.
Early childhood	Early childhood refers to the developmental period extending from the end of infancy to about 5 or 6 years of age; sometimes called the preschool years.
Trauma	Trauma refers to a severe physical injury or wound to the body caused by an external force, or a psychological shock having a lasting effect on mental life.
Society	The social sciences use the term society to mean a group of people that form a semi-closed (or semi-open) social system, in which most interactions are with other individuals belonging to the group.
Pleasure principle	The pleasure principle is the tendency to seek pleasure and avoid pain. In Freud's theory, this principle rules the Id, but is at least partly repressed by the reality principle.
Instinct	Instinct is the word used to describe inherent dispositions towards particular actions. They are generally an inherited pattern of responses or reactions to certain kinds of situations.
Anatomy	Anatomy is the branch of biology that deals with the structure and organization of living things. It can be divided into animal anatomy (zootomy) and plant anatomy (phytonomy). Major branches of anatomy include comparative anatomy, histology, and human anatomy.
Validity	The extent to which a test measures what it is intended to measure is called validity.
Innate	Innate behavior is not learned or influenced by the environment, rather, it is present or predisposed at birth.
Genetics	Genetics is the science of genes, heredity, and the variation of organisms.
Sexual abuse	Sexual abuse is a term used to describe non- consentual sexual relations between two or more parties which are considered criminally and/or morally offensive.
Attitude	An enduring mental representation of a person, place, or thing that evokes an emotional response and related behavior is called attitude.
Stimulus	A change in an environmental condition that elicits a response is a stimulus.
Compulsion	An apparently irresistible urge to repeat an act or engage in ritualistic behavior such as hand washing is referred to as a compulsion.
Affect	A subjective feeling or emotional tone often accompanied by bodily expressions noticeable to others is called affect.
Need for Power	Need for Power is a term introduced by David McClelland referring to an individual's need to be in charge. There are two kinds of power, social and personal.
Attention	Attention is the cognitive process of selectively concentrating on one thing while ignoring other things. Psychologists have labeled three types of attention: sustained attention, selective attention, and divided attention.
Friendship	The essentials of friendship are reciprocity and commitment between individuals who see themselves more or less as equals. Interaction between friends rests on a more equal power base than the interaction between children and adults.
Autonomy	Autonomy is the condition of something that does not depend on anything else.
Intrapsychic conflict	In psychoanalysis, the struggles among the id, ego, and superego are an intrapsychic conflict.

Go to **Cram101.com** for the Practice Tests for this Chapter.

Acquisition	Acquisition is the process of adapting to the environment, learning or becoming conditioned. In classical conditoning terms, it is the initial learning of the stimulus response link, which involves a neutral stimulus being associated with a unconditioned stimulus and becoming a conditioned stimulus.
Perception	Perception is the process of acquiring, interpreting, selecting, and organizing sensory information.
Chronic	Chronic refers to a relatively long duration, usually more than a few months.
Acute	Acute means sudden, sharp, and abrupt. Usually short in duration.
Suicide	Suicide behavior is rare in childhood but escalates in adolescence. The suicide rate increases in a linear fashion from adolescence through late adulthood.
Oedipus complex	The Oedipus complex is a concept developed by Sigmund Freud to explain the maturation of the infant boy through identification with the father and desire for the mother.
Penis	The penis is the external male copulatory organ and the external male organ of urination. In humans, the penis is homologous to the female clitoris, as it develops from the same embryonic structure. It is capable of erection for use in copulation.
Masculinity	Masculinity is a culturally determined value reflecting the set of characteristics of maleness.
Femininity	Femininity is the set of characteristics defined by a culture for idealized females.
Paradoxical	Paradoxical intention refers to instructing clients to do the opposite of the desired behavior. Telling an impotent man not to have sex or an insomniac not to sleep reduces anxiety to perform.
Psychotherapy	Psychotherapy is a set of techniques based on psychological principles intended to improve mental health, emotional or behavioral issues. Commonly psychotherapy involves a therapist and client(s), who discuss their issues in an effort to discover what they are and how they can solve them.
Free association	In psychoanalysis, the uncensored uttering of all thoughts that come to mind is called free association.
Altruism	Altruism is being helpful to other people with little or no interest in being rewarded for one's efforts. This is distinct from merely helping others.
Survey	A method of scientific investigation in which a large sample of people answer questions about their attitudes or behavior is referred to as a survey.
Questionnaire	A self-report method of data collection or clinical assessment method in which the individual being studied checks off items on a printed list, answers multiple-choice questions, or writes out answers to essay questions aimed at producing a selfdescription is called questionnaire.
Empathy	Empathy is the recognition and understanding of the states of mind, including beliefs, desires and particularly emotions of others without injecting your own.
Attitude scale	A multiple-item questionnaire designed to measure a person's attitude toward some object is called an attitude scale.
Neuroticism	Eysenck's use of the term neuroticism (or Emotional Stability) was proposed as the dimension describing individual differences in the predisposition towards neurotic disorder.
Extraversion	Extraversion, one of the big-five personailty traits, is marked by pronounced engagement with the external world. They are people who enjoy being with people, are full of energy, and often experience positive emotions.

Go to **Cram101.com** for the Practice Tests for this Chapter.

Agreeableness	Agreeableness, one of the big-five personality traits, reflects individual differences in concern with cooperation and social harmony. It is the degree individuals value getting along with others.
Openness to Experience	Openness to Experience, one of the big-five traits, describes a dimension of cognitive style that distinguishes imaginative, creative people from down-to-earth, conventional people.
Conscientiou-ness	Conscientiousness is one of the dimensions of the five-factor model of personality and individual differences involving being organized, thorough, and reliable as opposed to careless, negligent, and unreliable.
Discrimination	In Learning theory, discrimination refers the ability to distinguish between a conditioned stimulus and other stimuli. It can be brought about by extensive training or differential reinforcement. In social terms, it is the denial of privileges to a person or a group on the basis of prejudice.
Psychoanalytic theory	Psychoanalytic theory is a general term for approaches to psychoanalysis which attempt to provide a conceptual framework more-or-less independent of clinical practice rather than based on empirical analysis of clinical cases.
Falsifiability	According to Popper the extent to which a scientific assertion is amenable to systematic probes, any one of which could negate the scientist's expectations is referred to as falsifiability.
Parsimony	In science, parsimony is preference for the least complicated explanation for an observation. This is generally regarded as good when judging hypotheses. Occam's Razor also states the "principle of parsimony".
Teleology	While science investigates natural laws and phenomena, Philosophical naturalism and teleology investigate the existence or non-existence of an organizing principle behind those natural laws and phenomena. Philosophical naturalism asserts that there are no such principles. Teleology asserts that there are.
Causation	Causation concerns the time order relationship between two or more objects such that if a specific antecedent condition occurs the same consequent must always follow.
Motivation	In psychology, motivation is the driving force (desire) behind all actions of an organism.
Motives	Needs or desires that energize and direct behavior toward a goal are motives.
Social influence	Social influence is when the actions or thoughts of individual(s) are changed by other individual(s). Peer pressure is an example of social influence.

70

Go to **Cram101.com** for the Practice Tests for this Chapter.

Suicide	Suicide behavior is rare in childhood but escalates in adolescence. The suicide rate increases in a linear fashion from adolescence through late adulthood.
Humanistic	Humanistic refers to any system of thought focused on subjective experience and human problems and potentials.
Psychoanalysis	Psychoanalysis refers to the school of psychology that emphasizes the importance of unconscious motives and conflicts as determinants of human behavior. It was Freud's method of exploring human personality.
Reasoning	Reasoning is the act of using reason to derive a conclusion from certain premises. There are two main methods to reach a conclusion,deductive reasoning and inductive reasoning.
Personality	Personality refers to the pattern of enduring characteristics that differentiates a person, the patterns of behaviors that make each individual unique.
Karen Horney	Karen Horney, a neo-Freudian, deviated from orthodox Freudian analysis by emphasizing environmental and cultural, rather than biological, factors in neurosis.
Basic anxiety	Basic anxiety is a child's insecurity and doubt when a parent is indifferent, unloving, or disparaging. This anxiety, according to Horney, leads the child to a basic hostility toward his or her parents. The child may then become neurotic as an adult.
Anxiety	Anxiety is a complex combination of the feeling of fear, apprehension and worry often accompanied by physical sensations such as palpitations, chest pain and/or shortness of breath.
Theories	Theories are logically self-consistent models or frameworks describing the behavior of a certain natural or social phenomenon. They are broad explanations and predictions concerning phenomena of interest.
Psychodynamic	Most psychodynamic approaches are centered around the idea of a maladapted function developed early in life (usually childhood) which are at least in part unconscious. This maladapted function (a.k.a. defense mechanism) does not do well in place of a normal/healthy one.
Species	Species refers to a reproductively isolated breeding population.
Instinct	Instinct is the word used to describe inherent dispositions towards particular actions. They are generally an inherited pattern of responses or reactions to certain kinds of situations.
Evolution	Commonly used to refer to gradual change, evolution is the change in the frequency of alleles within a population from one generation to the next. This change may be caused by different mechanisms, including natural selection, genetic drift, or changes in population (gene flow).
Brain	The brain controls and coordinates most movement, behavior and homeostatic body functions such as heartbeat, blood pressure, fluid balance and body temperature. Functions of the brain are responsible for cognition, emotion, memory, motor learning and other sorts of learning. The brain is primarily made up of two types of cells: glia and neurons.
Human nature	Human nature is the fundamental nature and substance of humans, as well as the range of human behavior that is believed to be invariant over long periods of time and across very different cultural contexts.
Humanistic psychology	Humanistic psychology refers to the school of psychology that focuses on the uniqueness of human beings and their capacity for choice, growth, and psychological health.
Early childhood	Early childhood refers to the developmental period extending from the end of infancy to about 5 or 6 years of age; sometimes called the preschool years.
Sigmund Freud	Sigmund Freud was the founder of the psychoanalytic school, based on his theory that unconscious motives control much behavior, that particular kinds of unconscious thoughts and

Go to **Cram101.com** for the Practice Tests for this Chapter.

memories are the source of neurosis, and that neurosis could be treated through bringing these unconscious thoughts and memories to consciousness in psychoanalytic treatment.

Oedipus complex	The Oedipus complex is a concept developed by Sigmund Freud to explain the maturation of the infant boy through identification with the father and desire for the mother.
Adolescence	The period of life bounded by puberty and the assumption of adult responsibilities is adolescence.
Validity	The extent to which a test measures what it is intended to measure is called validity.
Psychoanalytic	Freud's theory that unconscious forces act as determinants of personality is called psychoanalytic theory. The theory is a developmental theory characterized by critical stages of development.
Sullivan	Sullivan developed the Self System, a configuration of the personality traits developed in childhood and reinforced by positive affirmation and the security operations developed in childhood to avoid anxiety and threats to self-esteem.
Rheumatoid arthritis	Rheumatoid arthritis is a chronic, inflammatory autoimmune disorder that causes the immune system to attack the joints. It is a disabling and painful inflammatory condition, which can lead to substantial loss of mobility due to pain and joint destruction.
Arthritis	Arthritis is a group of conditions that affect the health of the bone joints in the body. Arthritis can be caused from strains and injuries caused by repetitive motion, sports, overexertion, and falls. Unlike the autoimmune diseases, it largely affects older people and results from the degeneration of joint cartilage.
Trait	An enduring personality characteristic that tends to lead to certain behaviors is called a trait. The term trait also means a genetically inherited feature of an organism.
Authoritarian	The term authoritarian is used to describe a style that enforces strong and sometimes oppressive measures against those in its sphere of influence, generally without attempts at gaining their consent.
Society	The social sciences use the term society to mean a group of people that form a semi-closed (or semi-open) social system, in which most interactions are with other individuals belonging to the group.
Dichotomy	A dichotomy is the division of a proposition into two parts which are both mutually exclusive – i.e. both cannot be simultaneously true – and jointly exhaustive – i.e. they cover the full range of possible outcomes. They are often contrasting and spoken of as "opposites".
Life span	Life span refers to the upper boundary of life, the maximum number of years an individual can live. The maximum life span of human beings is about 120 years of age. Females live an average of 6 years longer than males.
Insanity	A legal status indicating that a person cannot be held responsible for his or her actions because of mental illness is called insanity.
Physiological needs	The easiest kinds of motivation to analyse, at least superficially, are those based upon obvious physiological needs. These include hunger, thirst, and escape from pain.
Individuality	According to Cooper, individuality consists of two dimensions: self-assertion and separateness.
Anatomy	Anatomy is the branch of biology that deals with the structure and organization of living things. It can be divided into animal anatomy (zootomy) and plant anatomy (phytonomy). Major branches of anatomy include comparative anatomy, histology, and human anatomy.
Fixation	Fixation in abnormal psychology is the state where an individual becomes obsessed with an

Go to **Cram101.com** for the Practice Tests for this Chapter.

attachment to another human, animal or inanimate object. Fixation in vision refers to maintaining the gaze in a constant direction. .

Social role	Social role refers to expected behavior patterns associated with particular social positions.
Sanity	Sanity considered as a legal term denotes that an individual is of sound mind and therefore can bear legal responsibility for his or her actions.
Motivation	In psychology, motivation is the driving force (desire) behind all actions of an organism.
Conformity	Conformity is the degree to which members of a group will change their behavior, views and attitudes to fit the views of the group. The group can influence members via unconscious processes or via overt social pressure on individuals.
Masochism	The counterpart of sadism is masochism, the sexual pleasure or gratification of having pain or suffering inflicted upon the self, often consisting of sexual fantasies or urges for being beaten, humiliated, bound, tortured, or otherwise made to suffer, either as an enhancement to or a substitute for sexual pleasure.
Sadism	Sadism is the sexual pleasure or gratification in the infliction of pain and suffering upon another person. It is considered to be a paraphilia. The word is derived from the name of the Marquis de Sade, a prolific French writer of sadistic novels.
Socialization	Social rules and social relations are created, communicated, and changed in verbal and nonverbal ways creating social complexity useful in identifying outsiders and intelligent breeding partners. The process of learning these skills is called socialization.
Assimilation	According to Piaget, assimilation is the process of the organism interacting with the environment given the organism's cognitive structure. Assimilation is reuse of schemas to fit new information.
Egocentrism	The inability to distinguish between one's own perspective and someone else's is referred to as egocentrism.
Creativity	Creativity is the ability to think about something in novel and unusual ways and come up with unique solutions to problems. It involves divergent thinking, having many solutions or views to a problem.
Creative self	According to Alfred Adler, the self-aware aspect of personality that strives to achieve its full potential is referred to as the creative self.
Passionate love	A state of intense absorption includes intense physiological arousal, psychological interest, and caring for the needs of another is referred to as passionate love.
Personality disorder	A mental disorder characterized by a set of inflexible, maladaptive personality traits that keep a person from functioning properly in society is referred to as a personality disorder.
Reflection	Reflection is the process of rephrasing or repeating thoughts and feelings expressed, making the person more aware of what they are saying or thinking.
Narcissism	Narcissism is the pattern of thinking and behaving which involves infatuation and obsession with one's self to the exclusion of others.
Hypochondriasis	The persistent beliefs that one has a medical disorder despite lack of medical findings are called hypochondriasis.
Attention	Attention is the cognitive process of selectively concentrating on one thing while ignoring other things. Psychologists have labeled three types of attention: sustained attention, selective attention, and divided attention.
Guilt	Guilt describes many concepts related to a negative emotion or condition caused by actions which are believed to be, morally wrong. According to Freud, the avoidance of guilt is the

	basis for moral behavior.
Depression	In everyday language depression refers to any downturn in mood, which may be relatively transitory and perhaps due to something trivial. This is differentiated from Clinical depression which is marked by symptoms that last two weeks or more and are so severe that they interfere with daily living.
Infancy	The developmental period that extends from birth to 18 or 24 months is called infancy.
Attachment	Attachment is the tendency to seek closeness to another person and feel secure when that person is present.
Syndrome	The term syndrome is the association of several clinically recognizable features, signs, symptoms, phenomena or characteristics which often occur together, so that the presence of one feature indicates the presence of the others.
Pathology	Pathology is the study of the processes underlying disease and other forms of illness, harmful abnormality, or dysfunction.
Psychotherapy	Psychotherapy is a set of techniques based on psychological principles intended to improve mental health, emotional or behavioral issues. Commonly psychotherapy involves a therapist and client(s), who discuss their issues in an effort to discover what they are and how they can solve them.
Transference	Transference is a phenomenon in psychology characterized by unconscious redirection of feelings from one person to another.
Countertrans-erence	Feelings that the psychoanalyst unconsciously directs to the analysis, stemming from his or her own emotional vulnerabilities and unresolved conflicts are countertransference effects.
Attitude	An enduring mental representation of a person, place, or thing that evokes an emotional response and related behavior is called attitude.
Psychohistory	Psychohistory is the study of the psychological motivations of historical events. It combines the insights of psychotherapy with the research methodology of the social sciences to understand the emotional origin of the social and political behavior of groups and nations, past and present.
Psychoanalyst	A psychoanalyst is a specially trained therapist who attempts to treat the individual by uncovering and revealing to the individual otherwise subconscious factors that are contributing to some undesirable behavor.
Motives	Needs or desires that energize and direct behavior toward a goal are motives.
Rorschach	The Rorschach inkblot test is a method of psychological evaluation. It is a projective test associated with the Freudian school of thought. Psychologists use this test to try to probe the unconscious minds of their patients.
Thematic Apperception Test	The Thematic Apperception Test uses a standard series of provocative yet ambiguous pictures about which the subject must tell a story. Each story is carefully analyzed to uncover underlying needs, attitudes, and patterns of reaction.
Questionnaire	A self-report method of data collection or clinical assessment method in which the individual being studied checks off items on a printed list, answers multiple-choice questions, or writes out answers to essay questions aimed at producing a selfdescription is called questionnaire.
Apperception	A newly experienced sensation is related to past experiences to form an understood situation. For Wundt, consciousness is composed of two "stages:" There is a large capacity working memory called the Blickfeld and the narrower consciousness called Apperception, or selective attention.

Population	Population refers to all members of a well-defined group of organisms, events, or things.
Mania	Mania is a medical condition characterized by severely elevated mood. Mania is most usually associated with bipolar disorder, where episodes of mania may cyclically alternate with episodes of depression.
Empirical	Empirical means the use of working hypotheses which are capable of being disproved using observation or experiment.
Insight	Insight refers to a sudden awareness of the relationships among various elements that had previously appeared to be independent of one another.
Determinism	Determinism is the philosophical proposition that every event, including human cognition and action, is causally determined by an unbroken chain of prior occurrences.
Free choice	Free choice refers to the ability to freely make choices that are not controlled by genetics, learning, or unconscious forces.
Teleology	While science investigates natural laws and phenomena, Philosophical naturalism and teleology investigate the existence or non-existence of an organizing principle behind those natural laws and phenonema. Philosophical naturalism asserts that there are no such principles. Teleology asserts that there are.
Causation	Causation concerns the time order relationship between two or more objects such that if a specific antecendent condition occurs the same consequent must always follow.
Social influence	Social influence is when the actions or thoughts of individual(s) are changed by other individual(s). Peer pressure is an example of social influence.

Go to **Cram101.com** for the Practice Tests for this Chapter.

Sullivan	Sullivan developed the Self System, a configuration of the personality traits developed in childhood and reinforced by positive affirmation and the security operations developed in childhood to avoid anxiety and threats to self-esteem.
Homosexual	Homosexual refers to a sexual orientation characterized by aesthetic attraction, romantic love, and sexual desire exclusively for members of the same sex or gender identity.
Psychiatrist	A psychiatrist is a physician who specializes in the diagnosis and treatment of psychological disorders.
Society	The social sciences use the term society to mean a group of people that form a semi-closed (or semi-open) social system, in which most interactions are with other individuals belonging to the group.
Prejudice	Prejudice in general, implies coming to a judgment on the subject before learning where the preponderance of the evidence actually lies, or formation of a judgement without direct experience.
Homosexuality	Homosexuality refers to a sexual orientation characterized by aesthetic attraction, romantic love, and sexual desire exclusively for members of the same sex or gender identity.
Personality	Personality refers to the pattern of enduring characteristics that differentiates a person, the patterns of behaviors that make each individual unique.
Construct	A generalized concept, such as anxiety or gravity, is a construct.
Context	In Psychology, context refers to the background stimuli that accompany some kind of foreground event.
Stages	Stages represent relatively discrete periods of time in which functioning is qualitatively different from functioning at other periods.
Late adolescence	Late adolescence refers to approximately the latter half of the second decade of life. Career interests, dating, and identity exploration are often more pronounced in late adolescence than in early adolescence.
Infancy	The developmental period that extends from birth to 18 or 24 months is called infancy.
Adolescence	The period of life bounded by puberty and the assumption of adult responsibilities is adolescence.
Anxiety	Anxiety is a complex combination of the feeling of fear, apprehension and worry often accompanied by physical sensations such as palpitations, chest pain and/or shortness of breath.
Crucial stage	Third of four of Jellinek's stages identified in the progression of alcoholism, is the crucial stage involving a loss of control of drinking and occasional binges of heavy drinking.
Theories	Theories are logically self-consistent models or frameworks describing the behavior of a certain natural or social phenomenon. They are broad explanations and predictions concerning phenomena of interest.
Psychodynamic	Most psychodynamic approaches are centered around the idea of a maladapted function developed early in life (usually childhood) which are at least in part unconscious. This maladapted function (a.k.a. defense mechanism) does not do well in place of a normal/healthy one.
Friendship	The essentials of friendship are reciprocity and commitment between individuals who see themselves more or less as equals. Interaction between friends rests on a more equal power base than the interaction between children and adults.
Schizophrenia	Schizophrenia is characterized by persistent defects in the perception or expression of

	reality. A person suffering from untreated schizophrenia typically demonstrates grossly disorganized thinking, and may also experience delusions or auditory hallucinations
Clinician	A health professional authorized to provide services to people suffering from one or more pathologies is a clinician.
Sympathetic	The sympathetic nervous system activates what is often termed the "fight or flight response". It is an automatic regulation system, that is, one that operates without the intervention of conscious thought.
Karen Horney	Karen Horney, a neo-Freudian, deviated from orthodox Freudian analysis by emphasizing environmental and cultural, rather than biological, factors in neurosis.
Psychoanalytic	Freud's theory that unconscious forces act as determinants of personality is called psychoanalytic theory. The theory is a developmental theory characterized by critical stages of development.
Sapir	Sapir proposed an alternative view of language in 1921, asserting that language influences the ways in which people think. Sapir's idea was adopted and developed during the 1940s by Whorf and eventually became the Sapir-Whorf Hypothesis.
Cerebral hemorrhage	Cerebral hemorrhage is a form of stroke that occurs when a blood vessel in the brain ruptures or bleeds. Hemorrhagic strokes are deadlier than their more common counterpart, ischemic strokes.
Jung	Jung was in some aspects a response to Sigmund Freud's psychoanalysis. He proposed and developed the concepts of the extroverted and introverted personality, archetypes, and the collective unconscious. His work has been influential in psychiatry and in the study of religion, literature, and related fields.
Overt behavior	An action or response that is directly observable and measurable is an overt behavior.
Empathy	Empathy is the recognition and understanding of the states of mind, including beliefs, desires and particularly emotions of others without injecting your own.
Blocking	If the one of the two members of a compound stimulus fails to produce the CR due to an earlier conditioning of the other member of the compound stimulus, blocking has occurred.
Perception	Perception is the process of acquiring, interpreting, selecting, and organizing sensory information.
Learning	Learning is a relatively permanent change in behavior that results from experience. Thus, to attribute a behavioral change to learning, the change must be relatively permanent and must result from experience.
Amnesia	Amnesia is a condition in which memory is disturbed. The causes of amnesia are organic or functional. Organic causes include damage to the brain, through trauma or disease, or use of certain (generally sedative) drugs.
Emotion	An emotion is a mental states that arise spontaneously, rather than through conscious effort. They are often accompanied by physiological changes.
Trait	An enduring personality characteristic that tends to lead to certain behaviors is called a trait. The term trait also means a genetically inherited feature of an organism.
Habit	A habit is a response that has become completely separated from its eliciting stimulus. Early learning theorists used the term to describe S-R associations, however not all S-R associations become a habit, rather many are extinguished after reinforcement is withdrawn.
Genitals	Genitals refers to the internal and external reproductive organs.
Attitude	An enduring mental representation of a person, place, or thing that evokes an emotional

Go to **Cram101.com** for the Practice Tests for this Chapter.

	response and related behavior is called attitude.
Puberty	Puberty refers to the process of physical changes by which a child's body becomes an adult body capable of reproduction.
Dissociation	Dissociation is a psychological state or condition in which certain thoughts, emotions, sensations, or memories are separated from the rest.
Punishment	Punishment is the addtion of a stimulus that reduces the frequency of a response, or the removal of a stimulus that results in a reduction of the response.
Sensation	Sensation is the first stage in the chain of biochemical and neurologic events that begins with the impinging of a stimulus upon the receptor cells of a sensory organ, which then leads to perception, the mental state that is reflected in statements like "I see a uniformly blue wall."
Cognition	The intellectual processes through which information is obtained, transformed, stored, retrieved, and otherwise used is cognition.
Subjective experience	Subjective experience refers to reality as it is perceived and interpreted, not as it exists objectively.
Threshold	In general, a threshold is a fixed location or value where an abrupt change is observed. In the sensory modalities, it is the minimum amount of stimulus energy necessary to elicit a sensory response.
Apathy	Apathy is the lack of emotion, motivation, or enthusiasm. Apathy is a psychological term for a state of indifference — where an individual is unresponsive or "indifferent" to aspects of emotional, social, or physical life. Clinical apathy is considered to be at an elevated level, while a moderate level might be considered depression, and an extreme level could be diagnosed as a dissociative disorder.
Pathology	Pathology is the study of the processes underlying disease and other forms of illness, harmful abnormality, or dysfunction.
Acculturation	Acculturation is the obtainment of culture by an individual or a group of people.
Socialization	Social rules and social relations are created, communicated, and changed in verbal and nonverbal ways creating social complexity useful in identifying outsiders and intelligent breeding partners. The process of learning these skills is called socialization.
Discrimination	In Learning theory, discrimination refers the ability to distinguish between a conditioned stimulus and other stimuli. It can be brought about by extensive training or differential reinforcement. In social terms, it is the denial of privileges to a person or a group on the basis of prejudice.
Egocentrism	The inability to distinguish between one's own perspective and someone else's is referred to as egocentrism.
Infatuation	The term "infatuation" carries connotations of immaturity or fatuousness, while "limerence" is intended to separate these connotations from the emotion.
Chronological age	Chronological age refers to the number of years that have elapsed since a person's birth.
Psychotherapy	Psychotherapy is a set of techniques based on psychological principles intended to improve mental health, emotional or behavioral issues. Commonly psychotherapy involves a therapist and client(s), who discuss their issues in an effort to discover what they are and how they can solve them.
Paraprofessional	A paraprofessional is an individual lacking a doctoral degree but trained to perform certain

Go to **Cram101.com** for the Practice Tests for this Chapter.

	functions usually reserved for clinicians.
Psychosis	Psychosis is a generic term for mental states in which the components of rational thought and perception are severely impaired. Persons experiencing a psychosis may experience hallucinations, hold paranoid or delusional beliefs, demonstrate personality changes and exhibit disorganized thinking. This is usually accompanied by features such as a lack of insight into the unusual or bizarre nature of their behavior, difficulties with social interaction and impairments in carrying out the activities of daily living.
Affect	A subjective feeling or emotional tone often accompanied by bodily expressions noticeable to others is called affect.
Introjection	Introjection is a psychological process where the subject replicates in itself behaviors, attributes or other fragments of the surrounding world, especially of other subjects. Cognate concepts are identification, incorporation and internalization.
Clinical psychologist	A psychologist, usually with a Ph.D, whose training is in the diagnosis, treatment, or research of psychological and behavioral disorders is a clinical psychologist.
Early childhood	Early childhood refers to the developmental period extending from the end of infancy to about 5 or 6 years of age; sometimes called the preschool years.
Sexual abuse	Sexual abuse is a term used to describe non- consentual sexual relations between two or more parties which are considered criminally and/or morally offensive.
Variable	A variable refers to a measurable factor, characteristic, or attribute of an individual or a system.
Depression	In everyday language depression refers to any downturn in mood, which may be relatively transitory and perhaps due to something trivial. This is differentiated from Clinical depression which is marked by symptoms that last two weeks or more and are so severe that they interfere with daily living.
Arousal	Arousal is a physiological and psychological state involving the activation of the reticular activating system in the brain stem, the autonomic nervous system and the endocrine system, leading to increased heart rate and blood pressure and a condition of alertness and readiness to respond.
Erik Erikson	Erik Erikson conceived eight stages of development, each confronting the individual with its own psychosocial demands, that continued into old age. Personality development, according to Erikson, takes place through a series of crises that must be overcome and internalized by the individual in preparation for the next developmental stage. Such crisis are not catastrophes but vulnerabilities.
Adler	Adler argued that human personality could be explained teleologically, separate strands dominated by the guiding purpose of the individual's unconscious self ideal to convert feelings of inferiority to superiority (or rather completeness). The desires of the self ideal were countered by social and ethical demands.
Postulates	Postulates are general statements about behavior that cannot be directly verified. They are used to generate theorems which can be tested.
Hypothesis	A specific statement about behavior or mental processes that is testable through research is a hypothesis.
Instinct	Instinct is the word used to describe inherent dispositions towards particular actions. They are generally an inherited pattern of responses or reactions to certain kinds of situations.
Illusion	An illusion is a distortion of a sensory perception.
Individuality	According to Cooper, individuality consists of two dimensions: self-assertion and

Go to **Cram101.com** for the Practice Tests for this Chapter.

separateness.

Social influence   Social influence is when the actions or thoughts of individual(s) are changed by other individual(s). Peer pressure is an example of social influence.

Identity crisis	Erikson coinded the term identity crisis: "...a psychosocial state or condition of disorientation and role confusion occurring especially in adolescents as a result of conflicting internal and external experiences, pressures, and expectations and often producing acute anxiety."
Erik Erikson	Erik Erikson conceived eight stages of development, each confronting the individual with its own psychosocial demands, that continued into old age. Personality development, according to Erikson, takes place through a series of crises that must be overcome and internalized by the individual in preparation for the next developmental stage. Such crisis are not catastrophes but vulnerabilities.
Psychoanalysis	Psychoanalysis refers to the school of psychology that emphasizes the importance of unconscious motives and conflicts as determinants of human behavior. It was Freud's method of exploring human personality.
Psychohistory	Psychohistory is the study of the psychological motivations of historical events. It combines the insights of psychotherapy with the research methodology of the social sciences to understand the emotional origin of the social and political behavior of groups and nations, past and present.
Stages	Stages represent relatively discrete periods of time in which functioning is qualitatively different from functioning at other periods.
Personality	Personality refers to the pattern of enduring characteristics that differentiates a person, the patterns of behaviors that make each individual unique.
Psychodynamic	Most psychodynamic approaches are centered around the idea of a maladapted function developed early in life (usually childhood) which are at least in part unconscious. This maladapted function (a.k.a. defense mechanism) does not do well in place of a normal/healthy one.
Adolescence	The period of life bounded by puberty and the assumption of adult responsibilities is adolescence.
Theories	Theories are logically self-consistent models or frameworks describing the behavior of a certain natural or social phenomenon. They are broad explanations and predictions concerning phenomena of interest.
Psychosexual stages	In Freudian theory each child passes through five psychosexual stages. During each stage, the id focuses on a distinct erogenous zone on the body. Suffering from trauma during any of the first three stages may result in fixation in that stage. Freud related the resolutions of the stages with adult personalities and personality disorders.
Reflection	Reflection is the process of rephrasing or repeating thoughts and feelings expressed, making the person more aware of what they are saying or thinking.
Late adolescence	Late adolescence refers to approximately the latter half of the second decade of life. Career interests, dating, and identity exploration are often more pronounced in late adolescence than in early adolescence.
Psychoanalyst	A psychoanalyst is a specially trained therapist who attempts to treat the individual by uncovering and revealing to the individual otherwise subconscious factors that are contributing to some undesirable behavor.
Anna Freud	Anna Freud was a pioneer of child psychoanalysis. She popularized the notion that adolescence is a period that includes rapid mood fluctuation with enormous uncertainty about self.
Psychoanalytic	Freud's theory that unconscious forces act as determinants of personality is called psychoanalytic theory. The theory is a developmental theory characterized by critical stages of development.

Go to **Cram101.com** for the Practice Tests for this Chapter.

Clinician	A health professional authorized to provide services to people suffering from one or more pathologies is a clinician.
Ego	In Freud's view the Ego serves to balance our primitive needs and our moral beliefs and taboos. Relying on experience, a healthy Ego provides the ability to adapt to reality and interact with the outside world.
Society	The social sciences use the term society to mean a group of people that form a semi-closed (or semi-open) social system, in which most interactions are with other individuals belonging to the group.
Analogy	An analogy is a comparison between two different things, in order to highlight some form of similarity. Analogy is the cognitive process of transferring information from a particular subject to another particular subject.
Individuality	According to Cooper, individuality consists of two dimensions: self-assertion and separateness.
Personal identity	The portion of the self-concept that pertains to the self as a distinct, separate individual is called personal identity.
Ego ideal	The component of the superego that involves ideal standards approved by parents is called ego ideal. The ego ideal rewards the child by conveying a sense of pride and personal value when the child acts according to ideal standards.
Social role	Social role refers to expected behavior patterns associated with particular social positions.
Trait	An enduring personality characteristic that tends to lead to certain behaviors is called a trait. The term trait also means a genetically inherited feature of an organism.
Ethnocentrism	Ethnocentrism is the tendency to look at the world primarily from the perspective of one's own culture.
Species	Species refers to a reproductively isolated breeding population.
Illusion	An illusion is a distortion of a sensory perception.
Perception	Perception is the process of acquiring, interpreting, selecting, and organizing sensory information.
Embryo	A developed zygote that has a rudimentary heart, brain, and other organs is referred to as an embryo.
Liver	The liver plays a major role in metabolism and has a number of functions in the body including detoxification, glycogen storage and plasma protein synthesis. It also produces bile, which is important for digestion. The liver converts most carbohydrates, proteing, and fats into glucose.
Critical period	A period of time when an innate response can be elicited by a particular stimulus is referred to as the critical period.
Psychosocial development	Erikson's psychosocial development describe eight developmental stages through which a healthily developing human should pass from infancy to late adulthood. In each stage the person confronts, and hopefully masters, new challenges.
Psychosocial stages	Erikson's eight developmental stages through the life span, each defined by a conflict that must be resolved satisfactorily in order for healthy personality development to occur are called psychosocial stages.
Maladaptive	In psychology, a behavior or trait is adaptive when it helps an individual adjust and function well within their social environment. A maladaptive behavior or trait is counterproductive to the individual.

95

Infancy	The developmental period that extends from birth to 18 or 24 months is called infancy.
Basic trust versus basic mistrust	Erikson's first stage, when infants develop trust or mistrust based on the quality of care, love, and affection provided is called the basic trust versus basic mistrust stage.
Lungs	The lungs are the essential organs of respiration. Its principal function is to transport oxygen from the atmosphere into the bloodstream, and excrete carbon dioxide from the bloodstream into the atmosphere.
Early childhood	Early childhood refers to the developmental period extending from the end of infancy to about 5 or 6 years of age; sometimes called the preschool years.
Primary caregiver	Primary caregiver refers to a person primarily responsible for the care of an infant, usually the infant's mother or father.
Depression	In everyday language depression refers to any downturn in mood, which may be relatively transitory and perhaps due to something trivial. This is differentiated from Clinical depression which is marked by symptoms that last two weeks or more and are so severe that they interfere with daily living.
Pathology	Pathology is the study of the processes underlying disease and other forms of illness, harmful abnormality, or dysfunction.
Anal stage	The anal stage in psychology is the term used by Sigmund Freud to describe the development during the second year of life, in which a child's pleasure and conflict centers are in the anal area.
Erogenous zone	An erogenous zone is an area of the human body that has heightened sensitivity and stimulation normally results in sexual response.
Learning	Learning is a relatively permanent change in behavior that results from experience. Thus, to attribute a behavioral change to learning, the change must be relatively permanent and must result from experience.
Autonomy	Autonomy is the condition of something that does not depend on anything else.
Autonomy versus shame and doubt	In Erikson's second stage of development, autonomy versus shame and doubt, which occurs in late infancy and toddlerhood, infants begin to discover that their behavior is their own.
Free will	The idea that human beings are capable of freely making choices or decisions is free will.
Compulsion	An apparently irresistible urge to repeat an act or engage in ritualistic behavior such as hand washing is referred to as a compulsion.
Oedipus complex	The Oedipus complex is a concept developed by Sigmund Freud to explain the maturation of the infant boy through identification with the father and desire for the mother.
Prototype	A concept of a category of objects or events that serves as a good example of the category is called a prototype.
Castration	Castration is any action, surgical, chemical or otherwise, by which a biological male loses use of the testes. This causes sterilization, i.e. prevents him from reproducing; it also greatly reduces the production of certain hormones, such as testosterone.
Penis	The penis is the external male copulatory organ and the external male organ of urination. In humans, the penis is homologous to the female clitoris, as it develops from the same embryonic structure. It is capable of erection for use in copulation.
Anxiety	Anxiety is a complex combination of the feeling of fear, apprehension and worry often accompanied by physical sensations such as palpitations, chest pain and/or shortness of breath.

Go to **Cram101.com** for the Practice Tests for this Chapter.

Sexual abuse	Sexual abuse is a term used to describe non- consentual sexual relations between two or more parties which are considered criminally and/or morally offensive.
Infantile sexuality	Freud's insistence that sexuality does not begin with adolescence, that babies are sexual too, is referred to as infantile sexuality.
Guilt	Guilt describes many concepts related to a negative emotion or condition caused by actions which are believed to be, morally wrong. According to Freud, the avoidance of guilt is the basis for moral behavior.
Initiative versus guilt	Initiative versus guilt is Erikson's third stage of development, which occurs during the preschool years. As preschool children encounter a widening social world, they are challenged more than they were as infants.
Latency	In child development, latency refers to a phase of psychosexual development characterized by repression of sexual impulses. In learning theory, latency is the delay between stimulus (S) and response (R), which according to Hull depends on the strength of the association.
Industry versus inferiority	Erikson's fourth stage of development, industry versus inferiority, develops in the elementary school years. Initiative brings children into contact with a new experiences. They direct their energy toward mastering knowledge and intellectual skills.
Adler	Adler argued that human personality could be explained teleologically, separate strands dominated by the guiding purpose of the individual's unconscious self ideal to convert feelings of inferiority to superiority (or rather completeness). The desires of the self ideal were countered by social and ethical demands.
Puberty	Puberty refers to the process of physical changes by which a child's body becomes an adult body capable of reproduction.
Identity versus identity confusion	Identity versus identity confusion is Erikson's fifth developmental stage, which individuals experience during the adolescent years. At this time, individuals are faced with finding out who they are, what they re all about, and where they are going in life.
Trial and error	Trial and error is an approach to problem solving in which one solution after another is tried in no particular order until an answer is found.
Conformity	Conformity is the degree to which members of a group will change their behavior, views and attitudes to fit the views of the group. The group can influence members via unconscious processes or via overt social pressure on individuals.
Context	In Psychology, context refers to the background stimuli that accompany some kind of foreground event.
Shaping	The concept of reinforcing successive, increasingly accurate approximations to a target behavior is called shaping. The target behavior is broken down into a hierarchy of elemental steps, each step more sophisticated then the last. By successively reinforcing each of the the elemental steps, a form of differential reinforcement, until that step is learned while extinguishing the step below, the target behavior is gradually achieved.
Syndrome	The term syndrome is the association of several clinically recognizable features, signs, symptoms, phenomena or characteristics which often occur together, so that the presence of one feature indicates the presence of the others.
Regression	Return to a form of behavior characteristic of an earlier stage of development is called regression.
Ideology	An ideology can be thought of as a comprehensive vision, as a way of looking at things, as in common sense and several philosophical tendencies, or a set of ideas proposed by the dominant class of a society to all members of this society.

Generativity	Generativity refers to an adult's concern for and commitment to the well-being of future generations.
Acquisition	Acquisition is the process of adapting to the environment, learning or becoming conditioned. In classical conditoning terms, it is the initial learning of the stimulus response link, which involves a neutral stimulus being associated with a unconditioned stimulus and becoming a conditioned stimulus.
Intimacy versus isolation	The life crisis of young adulthood, which is characterized by the task of developing binding intimate relationships is referred to as Erikson's intimacy versus isolation stage.
Infatuation	The term "infatuation" carries connotations of immaturity or fatuousness, while "limerence" is intended to separate these connotations from the emotion.
Friendship	The essentials of friendship are reciprocity and commitment between individuals who see themselves more or less as equals. Interaction between friends rests on a more equal power base than the interaction between children and adults.
Creativity	Creativity is the ability to think about something in novel and unusual ways and come up with unique solutions to problems. It involves divergent thinking, having many solutions or views to a problem.
Integrity versus despair	Erikson's eighth and final stage of development is Integrity Versus Despair. In late adulthood individuals reflect on the past and either piece together a positive review or conclude that one's life has not been well spent.
Wisdom	Wisdom is the ability to make correct judgments and decisions. It is an intangible quality gained through experience. Whether or not something is wise is determined in a pragmatic sense by its popularity, how long it has been around, and its ability to predict against future events.
Attitude	An enduring mental representation of a person, place, or thing that evokes an emotional response and related behavior is called attitude.
Generalization	In conditioning, the tendency for a conditioned response to be evoked by stimuli that are similar to the stimulus to which the response was conditioned is a generalization. The greater the similarity among the stimuli, the greater the probability of generalization.
Apathy	Apathy is the lack of emotion, motivation, or enthusiasm. Apathy is a psychological term for a state of indifference — where an individual is unresponsive or "indifferent" to aspects of emotional, social, or physical life. Clinical apathy is considered to be at an elevated level, while a moderate level might be considered depression, and an extreme level could be diagnosed as a dissociative disorder.
Attention	Attention is the cognitive process of selectively concentrating on one thing while ignoring other things. Psychologists have labeled three types of attention: sustained attention, selective attention, and divided attention.
Empirical	Empirical means the use of working hypotheses which are capable of being disproved using observation or experiment.
Mentoring	Mentoring refers to a developmental relationship between a more experienced individual and a less experienced partner sometimes referred to as a protégé. In well-designed formal mentoring programs, there are program goals, schedules, and training.
Reasoning	Reasoning is the act of using reason to derive a conclusion from certain premises. There are two main methods to reach a conclusion,deductive reasoning and inductive reasoning.
Moral reasoning	Moral reasoning involves concepts of justice, whereas social conventional judgments are concepts of social organization.

Go to **Cram101.com** for the Practice Tests for this Chapter.

Agentic	"The core features of agency enable people to play a part in their self-development, adaptation, and self-renewal with changing times, " Bandura's agentic perspective of social cognitive theory. The person is active in the process.
Median	The median is a number that separates the higher half of a sample, a population, or a probability distribution from the lower half. It is the middle value in a distribution, above and below which lie an equal number of values.
Falsifiability	According to Popper the extent to which a scientific assertion is amenable to systematic probes, any one of which could negate the scientist's expectations is referred to as falsifiability.
Motivation	In psychology, motivation is the driving force (desire) behind all actions of an organism.
Gerontology	Gerontology is the study of the elderly, and of the aging process itself. It is to be distinguished from geriatrics, which is the study of the diseases of the elderly. Gerontology covers the social, psychological and biology aspects of aging.
Generativity versus stagnation	Generativity versus stagnation is Erikson's term for the crisis of middle adulthood. The individual is characterized by the task of being productive and contributing to younger generations.
Counselor	A counselor is a mental health professional who specializes in helping people with problems not involving serious mental disorders.
Parsimony	In science, parsimony is preference for the least complicated explanation for an observation. This is generally regarded as good when judging hypotheses. Occam's Razor also states the "principle of parsimony".
Anatomy	Anatomy is the branch of biology that deals with the structure and organization of living things. It can be divided into animal anatomy (zootomy) and plant anatomy (phytonomy). Major branches of anatomy include comparative anatomy, histology, and human anatomy.
Socialization	Social rules and social relations are created, communicated, and changed in verbal and nonverbal ways creating social complexity useful in identifying outsiders and intelligent breeding partners. The process of learning these skills is called socialization.
Temperament	Temperament refers to a basic, innate disposition to change behavior. The activity level is an important dimension of temperament.
Free choice	Free choice refers to the ability to freely make choices that are not controlled by genetics, learning, or unconscious forces.
Teleology	While science investigates natural laws and phenomena, Philosophical naturalism and teleology investigate the existence or non-existence of an organizing principle behind those natural laws and phenomena. Philosophical naturalism asserts that there are no such principles. Teleology asserts that there are.
Causation	Causation concerns the time order relationship between two or more objects such that if a specific antecendent condition occurs the same consequent must always follow.
Individual differences	Individual differences psychology studies the ways in which individual people differ in their behavior. This is distinguished from other aspects of psychology in that although psychology is ostensibly a study of individuals, modern psychologists invariably study groups.
Trust versus mistrust	In Erikson's first stage of psychosexual development, trust versus mistrust, children do-or do not-come to trust that primary caregivers and the environment will meet their needs. The first year of life is the key time for the development of attachment.
Psychosexual development	In psychodynamic theory, the process by which libidinal energy is expressed through different erogenous zones during different stages of development is called psychosexual development.

| Crucial stage | Third of four of Jellinek's stages identified in the progression of alcoholism, is the crucial stage involving a loss of control of drinking and occasional binges of heavy drinking. |

IQ test	An IQ test is a standardized test developed to measure a person's cognitive abilities ("intelligence") in relation to their age group.
Maslow	Maslow is mostly noted today for his proposal of a hierarchy of human needs which he often presented as a pyramid. Maslow was an instrumental player in the formation of the humanistic movement, also known as the third force in psychology.
Humanistic	Humanistic refers to any system of thought focused on subjective experience and human problems and potentials.
Humanistic psychology	Humanistic psychology refers to the school of psychology that focuses on the uniqueness of human beings and their capacity for choice, growth, and psychological health.
Rollo May	Rollo May was the best known American existential psychologist, authoring the influential book Love and Will in 1969. He differs from other humanistic psychologists in showing a sharper awareness of the tragic dimensions of human existence.
Theories	Theories are logically self-consistent models or frameworks describing the behavior of a certain natural or social phenomenon. They are broad explanations and predictions concerning phenomena of interest.
Carl Rogers	Carl Rogers was instrumental in the development of non-directive psychotherapy, also known as "client-centered" psychotherapy. Rogers' basic tenets were unconditional positive regard, genuineness, and empathic understanding, with each demonstrated by the counselor.
Allport	Allport was a trait theorist. Those traits he believed to predominate a person's personality were called central traits. Traits such that one could be indentifed by the trait, were referred to as cardinal traits. Central traits and cardinal traits are influenced by environmental factors.
Psychoanalysis	Psychoanalysis refers to the school of psychology that emphasizes the importance of unconscious motives and conflicts as determinants of human behavior. It was Freud's method of exploring human personality.
Behaviorism	The school of psychology that defines psychology as the study of observable behavior and studies relationships between stimuli and responses is called behaviorism. Behaviorism relied heavily on animal research and stated the same principles governed the behavior of both nonhumans and humans.
Watson	Watson, the father of behaviorism, developed the term "Behaviorism" as a name for his proposal to revolutionize the study of human psychology in order to put it on a firm experimental footing.
Shyness	A tendency to avoid others plus uneasiness and strain when socializing is called shyness.
Depression	In everyday language depression refers to any downturn in mood, which may be relatively transitory and perhaps due to something trivial. This is differentiated from Clinical depression which is marked by symptoms that last two weeks or more and are so severe that they interfere with daily living.
Reflection	Reflection is the process of rephrasing or repeating thoughts and feelings expressed, making the person more aware of what they are saying or thinking.
Punishment	Punishment is the addtion of a stimulus that reduces the frequency of a response, or the removal of a stimulus that results in a reduction of the response.
Attitude	An enduring mental representation of a person, place, or thing that evokes an emotional response and related behavior is called attitude.
Intellectually gifted	Intellectually gifted refers to having an IQ score above 130; about 2 to 4 percent of the population.

Social skills	Social skills are skills used to interact and communicate with others to assist status in the social structure and other motivations.
Titchener	Titchener attempted to classify the structures of the mind, not unlike the way a chemist breaks down chemicals into their component parts-water into hydrogen and oxygen for example. He conceived of hydrogen and oxygen as structures of a chemical compound, and sensations and thoughts as structures of the mind. This approach became known as structuralism.
Harlow	Harlow and his famous wire and cloth surrogate mother monkey studies demonstrated that the need for affection created a stronger bond between mother and infant than did physical needs. He also found that the more discrimination problems the monkeys solved, the better they became at solving them.
Prejudice	Prejudice in general, implies coming to a judgment on the subject before learning where the preponderance of the evidence actually lies, or formation of a judgement without direct experience.
Thorndike	Thorndike worked in animal behavior and the learning process leading to the theory of connectionism. Among his most famous contributions were his research on cats escaping from puzzle boxes, and his formulation of the Law of Effect.
Intelligence test	An intelligence test is a standardized means of assessing a person's current mental ability, for example, the Stanford-Binet test and the Wechsler Adult Intelligence Scale.
Adler	Adler argued that human personality could be explained teleologically, separate strands dominated by the guiding purpose of the individual's unconscious self ideal to convert feelings of inferiority to superiority (or rather completeness). The desires of the self ideal were countered by social and ethical demands.
Rotter	Rotter focused on the application of social learning theory (SLT) to clinical psychology. She introduced the ideas of learning from generalized expectancies of reinforcement and internal/external locus of control (self-initiated change versus change influenced by others). According to Rotter, health outcomes could be improved by the development of a sense of personal control over one's life.
Chronic	Chronic refers to a relatively long duration, usually more than a few months.
Motivation	In psychology, motivation is the driving force (desire) behind all actions of an organism.
Species	Species refers to a reproductively isolated breeding population.
Friendship	The essentials of friendship are reciprocity and commitment between individuals who see themselves more or less as equals. Interaction between friends rests on a more equal power base than the interaction between children and adults.
Hierarchy of needs	Maslow's hierarchy of needs is often depicted as a pyramid consisting of five levels: the four lower levels are grouped together as deficiency needs, while the top level is termed being needs. While our deficiency needs must be met, our being needs are continually shaping our behavior.
Physiological needs	The easiest kinds of motivation to analyse, at least superficially, are those based upon obvious physiological needs. These include hunger, thirst, and escape from pain.
Society	The social sciences use the term society to mean a group of people that form a semi-closed (or semi-open) social system, in which most interactions are with other individuals belonging to the group.
Anxiety	Anxiety is a complex combination of the feeling of fear, apprehension and worry often accompanied by physical sensations such as palpitations, chest pain and/or shortness of breath.

Go to **Cram101.com** for the Practice Tests for this Chapter.

Perception	Perception is the process of acquiring, interpreting, selecting, and organizing sensory information.
Threshold	In general, a threshold is a fixed location or value where an abrupt change is observed. In the sensory modalities, it is the minimum amount of stimulus energy necessary to elicit a sensory response.
Pathology	Pathology is the study of the processes underlying disease and other forms of illness, harmful abnormality, or dysfunction.
Deprivation	Deprivation, is the loss or withholding of normal stimulation, nutrition, comfort, love, and so forth; a condition of lacking. The level of stimulation is less than what is required.
Compensation	In personaility, compensation, according to Adler, is an effort to overcome imagined or real inferiorities by developing one's abilities.
Maturation	The orderly unfolding of traits, as regulated by the genetic code is called maturation.
Reinforcement	In operant conditioning, reinforcement is any change in an environment that (a) occurs after the behavior, (b) seems to make that behavior re-occur more often in the future and (c) that reoccurence of behavior must be the result of the change.
Personality	Personality refers to the pattern of enduring characteristics that differentiates a person, the patterns of behaviors that make each individual unique.
Expressive behaviors	Behaviors that express or communicate emotion or personal feelings are expressive behaviors.
Malnutrition	Malnutrition is a general term for the medical condition in a person or animal caused by an unbalanced diet—either too little or too much food, or a diet missing one or more important nutrients.
Obsession	An obsession is a thought or idea that the sufferer cannot stop thinking about. Common examples include fears of acquiring disease, getting hurt, or causing harm to someone. They are typically automatic, frequent, distressing, and difficult to control or put an end to by themselves.
Learning	Learning is a relatively permanent change in behavior that results from experience. Thus, to attribute a behavioral change to learning, the change must be relatively permanent and must result from experience.
Wertheimer	His discovery of the phi phenomenon concerning the illusion of motion gave rise to the influential school of Gestalt psychology. In the latter part of his life, Wertheimer directed much of his attention to the problem of learning.
Syndrome	The term syndrome is the association of several clinically recognizable features, signs, symptoms, phenomena or characteristics which often occur together, so that the presence of one feature indicates the presence of the others.
Spinoza	Spinoza was a determinist who held that absolutely everything that happens occurs through the operation of necessity. All behavior is fully determined, freedom being our capacity to know we are determined and to understand why we act as we do.
William James	Functionalism as a psychology developed out of Pragmatism as a philosophy: To find the meaning of an idea, you have to look at its consequences. This led William James and his students towards an emphasis on cause and effect, prediction and control, and observation of environment and behavior, over the careful introspection of the Structuralists.
Possible self	What individuals might become, what they would like to become, and what they are afraid of becoming is called the possible self.

Go to **Cram101.com** for the Practice Tests for this Chapter.

Psychopathology	Psychopathology refers to the field concerned with the nature and development of mental disorders.
Psychosomatic	A psychosomatic illness is one with physical manifestations and perhaps a supposed psychological cause. It is often diagnosed when any known or identifiable physical cause was excluded by medical examination.
Dichotomy	A dichotomy is the division of a proposition into two parts which are both mutually exclusive – i.e. both cannot be simultaneously true – and jointly exhaustive – i.e. they cover the full range of possible outcomes. They are often contrasting and spoken of as "opposites".
Autonomy	Autonomy is the condition of something that does not depend on anything else.
Paranoia	In popular culture, the term paranoia is usually used to describe excessive concern about one's own well-being, sometimes suggesting a person holds persecutory beliefs concerning a threat to themselves or their property and is often linked to a belief in conspiracy theories.
Population	Population refers to all members of a well-defined group of organisms, events, or things.
Peak experiences	Temporary moments of self-actualization are peak experiences.
Ecstasy	Ecstasy as an emotion is to be outside oneself, in a trancelike state in which an individual transcends ordinary consciousness and as a result has a heightened capacity for exceptional thought or experience. Ecstasy also refers to a relatively new hallucinogen that is chemically similar to mescaline and the amphetamines.
Emotion	An emotion is a mental states that arise spontaneously, rather than through conscious effort. They are often accompanied by physiological changes.
Discrimination	In Learning theory, discrimination refers the ability to distinguish between a conditioned stimulus and other stimuli. It can be brought about by extensive training or differential reinforcement. In social terms, it is the denial of privileges to a person or a group on the basis of prejudice.
Creativity	Creativity is the ability to think about something in novel and unusual ways and come up with unique solutions to problems. It involves divergent thinking, having many solutions or views to a problem.
Heterogeneous	A heterogeneous compound, mixture, or other such object is one that consists of many different items, which are often not easily sorted or separated, though they are clearly distinct.
Research method	The scope of the research method is to produce some new knowledge. This, in principle, can take three main forms: Exploratory research; Constructive research; and Empirical research.
Sensation	Sensation is the first stage in the chain of biochemical and neurologic events that begins with the impinging of a stimulus upon the receptor cells of a sensory organ, which then leads to perception, the mental state that is reflected in statements like "I see a uniformly blue wall."
Construct	A generalized concept, such as anxiety or gravity, is a construct.
Validity	The extent to which a test measures what it is intended to measure is called validity.
Reliability	Reliability means the extent to which a test produces a consistent , reproducible score .
Likert scale	A Likert scale is a type of psychometric scale often used in questionnaires. It asks respondents to specify their level of agreement to each of a list of statements. It is a bipolar scaling method, measuring either positive and negative response to a statement.
Psychotherapy	Psychotherapy is a set of techniques based on psychological principles intended to improve

	mental health, emotional or behavioral issues. Commonly psychotherapy involves a therapist and client(s), who discuss their issues in an effort to discover what they are and how they can solve them.
Csikszentmihalyi	Csikszentmihalyi is noted for his work in the study of happiness, creativity, subjective well-being, and fun, but is best known for his having been the architect of the notion of flow: "... people are most happy when they are in a state of flow--a Zen-like state of total oneness...".
Wisdom	Wisdom is the ability to make correct judgments and decisions. It is an intangible quality gained through experience. Whether or not something is wise is determined in a pragmatic sense by its popularity, how long it has been around, and its ability to predict against future events.
Positive relationship	Statistically, a positive relationship refers to a mathematical relationship in which increases in one measure are matched by increases in the other.
Ego	In Freud's view the Ego serves to balance our primitive needs and our moral beliefs and taboos. Relying on experience, a healthy Ego provides the ability to adapt to reality and interact with the outside world.
Empirical	Empirical means the use of working hypotheses which are capable of being disproved using observation or experiment.
Life satisfaction	A person's attitudes about his or her overall life are referred to as life satisfaction.
Factor analysis	Factor analysis is a statistical technique that originated in psychometrics. The objective is to explain the most of the variability among a number of observable random variables in terms of a smaller number of unobservable random variables called factors.
Falsifiability	According to Popper the extent to which a scientific assertion is amenable to systematic probes, any one of which could negate the scientist's expectations is referred to as falsifiability.
Operational definition	An operational definition is the definition of a concept or action in terms of the observable and repeatable process, procedures, and appartaus that illustrates the concept or action.
Scientific method	Psychologists gather data in order to describe, understand, predict, and control behavior. Scientific method refers to an approach that can be used to discover accurate information. It includes these steps: understand the problem, collect data, draw conclusions, and revise research conclusions.
Human nature	Human nature is the fundamental nature and substance of humans, as well as the range of human behavior that is believed to be invariant over long periods of time and across very different cultural contexts.
Free choice	Free choice refers to the ability to freely make choices that are not controlled by genetics, learning, or unconscious forces.
Determinism	Determinism is the philosophical proposition that every event, including human cognition and action, is causally determined by an unbroken chain of prior occurrences.
Consciousness	The awareness of the sensations, thoughts, and feelings being experienced at a given moment is called consciousness.
Social influence	Social influence is when the actions or thoughts of individual(s) are changed by other individual(s). Peer pressure is an example of social influence.
Affect	A subjective feeling or emotional tone often accompanied by bodily expressions noticeable to others is called affect.

Go to **Cram101.com** for the Practice Tests for this Chapter.

Social skills	Social skills are skills used to interact and communicate with others to assist status in the social structure and other motivations.
Personality	Personality refers to the pattern of enduring characteristics that differentiates a person, the patterns of behaviors that make each individual unique.
Humanistic	Humanistic refers to any system of thought focused on subjective experience and human problems and potentials.
Carl Rogers	Carl Rogers was instrumental in the development of non-directive psychotherapy, also known as "client-centered" psychotherapy. Rogers' basic tenets were unconditional positive regard, genuineness, and empathic understanding, with each demonstrated by the counselor.
Empirical	Empirical means the use of working hypotheses which are capable of being disproved using observation or experiment.
Theories	Theories are logically self-consistent models or frameworks describing the behavior of a certain natural or social phenomenon. They are broad explanations and predictions concerning phenomena of interest.
Attitude	An enduring mental representation of a person, place, or thing that evokes an emotional response and related behavior is called attitude.
Psychoanalysis	Psychoanalysis refers to the school of psychology that emphasizes the importance of unconscious motives and conflicts as determinants of human behavior. It was Freud's method of exploring human personality.
Society	The social sciences use the term society to mean a group of people that form a semi-closed (or semi-open) social system, in which most interactions are with other individuals belonging to the group.
Otto Rank	Otto Rank extended psychoanalytic theory to the study of legend, myth, art, and other works of creativity. He favored a more egalitarian relationship with patients and is sometimes considered the forerunner of client-centered therapy.
Psychotherapy	Psychotherapy is a set of techniques based on psychological principles intended to improve mental health, emotional or behavioral issues. Commonly psychotherapy involves a therapist and client(s), who discuss their issues in an effort to discover what they are and how they can solve them.
Encounter group	A type of group that fosters self-awareness by focusing on how group members relate to one another in a setting that encourages open expression of feelings is called an encounter group.
Openness to Experience	Openness to Experience, one of the big-five traits, describes a dimension of cognitive style that distinguishes imaginative, creative people from down-to-earth, conventional people.
Shyness	A tendency to avoid others plus uneasiness and strain when socializing is called shyness.
Unconditional positive regard	Unqualified caring and nonjudgmental acceptance of another is called unconditional positive regard.
Empathy	Empathy is the recognition and understanding of the states of mind, including beliefs, desires and particularly emotions of others without injecting your own.
Hierarchy of needs	Maslow's hierarchy of needs is often depicted as a pyramid consisting of five levels: the four lower levels are grouped together as deficiency needs, while the top level is termed being needs. While our deficiency needs must be met, our being needs are continually shaping our behavior.
Friendship	The essentials of friendship are reciprocity and commitment between individuals who see

Go to **Cram101.com** for the Practice Tests for this Chapter.

themselves more or less as equals. Interaction between friends rests on a more equal power base than the interaction between children and adults.

Innate
Innate behavior is not learned or influenced by the environment, rather, it is present or predisposed at birth.

Anxiety
Anxiety is a complex combination of the feeling of fear, apprehension and worry often accompanied by physical sensations such as palpitations, chest pain and/or shortness of breath.

Symbolization
In Bandura's social cognitive theory, the ability to think about one's social behavior in terms of words and images is referred to as symbolization. Symbolization allows us to translate a transient experience into a guide for future action.

Consciousness
The awareness of the sensations, thoughts, and feelings being experienced at a given moment is called consciousness.

Perception
Perception is the process of acquiring, interpreting, selecting, and organizing sensory information.

Early childhood
Early childhood refers to the developmental period extending from the end of infancy to about 5 or 6 years of age; sometimes called the preschool years.

Denial
Denial is a psychological defense mechanism in which a person faced with a fact that is uncomfortable or painful to accept rejects it instead, insisting that it is not true despite what may be overwhelming evidence.

Empathic understanding
Empathic understanding refers to ability to perceive a client's feelings from the client's frame of reference.

Counselor
A counselor is a mental health professional who specializes in helping people with problems not involving serious mental disorders.

Hypothesis
A specific statement about behavior or mental processes that is testable through research is a hypothesis.

Sufficient condition
To say that A is a sufficient condition for B is to say precisely the converse: that A cannot occur without B, or whenever A occurs, B occurs. That there is a fire is sufficient for there being smoke.

Persona
In Jungian archetypal psychology, the Persona is the mask or appearance one presents to the world. It may appear in dreams under various guises.

Prejudice
Prejudice in general, implies coming to a judgment on the subject before learning where the preponderance of the evidence actually lies, or formation of a judgement without direct experience.

Projection
Attributing one's own undesirable thoughts, impulses, traits, or behaviors to others is referred to as projection.

Stages
Stages represent relatively discrete periods of time in which functioning is qualitatively different from functioning at other periods.

Reasoning
Reasoning is the act of using reason to derive a conclusion from certain premises. There are two main methods to reach a conclusion,deductive reasoning and inductive reasoning.

Maslow
Maslow is mostly noted today for his proposal of a hierarchy of human needs which he often presented as a pyramid. Maslow was an instrumental player in the formation of the humanistic movement, also known as the third force in psychology.

Human nature
Human nature is the fundamental nature and substance of humans, as well as the range of human behavior that is believed to be invariant over long periods of time and across very different

Go to **Cram101.com** for the Practice Tests for this Chapter.

cultural contexts.

Subjective experience	Subjective experience refers to reality as it is perceived and interpreted, not as it exists objectively.
Nurture	Nurture refers to the environmental influences on behavior due to nutrition, culture, socioeconomic status, and learning.
Infancy	The developmental period that extends from birth to 18 or 24 months is called infancy.
Creativity	Creativity is the ability to think about something in novel and unusual ways and come up with unique solutions to problems. It involves divergent thinking, having many solutions or views to a problem.
Thematic Apperception Test	The Thematic Apperception Test uses a standard series of provocative yet ambiguous pictures about which the subject must tell a story. Each story is carefully analyzed to uncover underlying needs, attitudes, and patterns of reaction.
Personality test	A personality test aims to describe aspects of a person's character that remain stable across situations.
Projective personality test	A method in which a person is shown an ambiguous stimulus and asked to describe it or tell a story about it is called a projective personality test.
Henry Murray	Henry Murray believed that personality could be better understood by investigating the unconscious mind. He is most famous for the development of the Thematic Apperception Test (TAT), a widely used projective measure of personality.
Ethnocentrism	Ethnocentrism is the tendency to look at the world primarily from the perspective of one's own culture.
Attitude scale	A multiple-item questionnaire designed to measure a person's attitude toward some object is called an attitude scale.
Apperception	A newly experienced sensation is related to past experiences to form an understood situation. For Wundt, consciousness is composed of two "stages:" There is a large capacity working memory called the Blickfeld and the narrower consciousness called Apperception, or selective attention.
Control group	A group that does not receive the treatment effect in an experiment is referred to as the control group or sometimes as the comparison group.
Attention	Attention is the cognitive process of selectively concentrating on one thing while ignoring other things. Psychologists have labeled three types of attention: sustained attention, selective attention, and divided attention.
Variance	The degree to which scores differ among individuals in a distribution of scores is the variance.
Depression	In everyday language depression refers to any downturn in mood, which may be relatively transitory and perhaps due to something trivial. This is differentiated from Clinical depression which is marked by symptoms that last two weeks or more and are so severe that they interfere with daily living.
Eating disorders	Psychological disorders characterized by distortion of the body image and gross disturbances in eating patterns are called eating disorders.
Affective	Affective is the way people react emotionally, their ability to feel another living thing's pain or joy.
Questionnaire	A self-report method of data collection or clinical assessment method in which the individual

Go to **Cram101.com** for the Practice Tests for this Chapter.

being studied checks off items on a printed list, answers multiple-choice questions, or writes out answers to essay questions aimed at producing a selfdescription is called questionnaire.

Baseline Measure of a particular behavior or process taken before the introduction of the independent variable or treatment is called the baseline.

Positive relationship Statistically, a positive relationship refers to a mathematical relationship in which increases in one measure are matched by increases in the other.

Learning Learning is a relatively permanent change in behavior that results from experience. Thus, to attribute a behavioral change to learning, the change must be relatively permanent and must result from experience.

Paradigm Paradigm refers to the set of practices that defines a scientific discipline during a particular period of time. It provides a framework from which to conduct research, it ensures that a certain range of phenomena, those on which the paradigm focuses, are explored thoroughly. Itmay also blind scientists to other, perhaps more fruitful, ways of dealing with their subject matter.

Group dynamics The term group dynamics implies that individual behaviors may differ depending on individuals' current or prospective connections to a sociological group.

Affect A subjective feeling or emotional tone often accompanied by bodily expressions noticeable to others is called affect.

Operational definition An operational definition is the definition of a concept or action in terms of the observable and repeatable process, procedures, and appartaus that illustrates the concept or action.

Skinner Skinner conducted research on shaping behavior through positive and negative reinforcement, and demonstrated operant conditioning, a technique which he developed in contrast with classical conditioning.

Free choice Free choice refers to the ability to freely make choices that are not controlled by genetics, learning, or unconscious forces.

Illusion An illusion is a distortion of a sensory perception.

Teleology While science investigates natural laws and phenomena, Philosophical naturalism and teleology investigate the existence or non-existence of an organizing principle behind those natural laws and phenomena. Philosophical naturalism asserts that there are no such principles. Teleology asserts that there are.

Individual differences Individual differences psychology studies the ways in which individual people differ in their behavior. This is distinguished from other aspects of psychology in that although psychology is ostensibly a study of individuals, modern psychologists invariably study groups.

Individuality According to Cooper, individuality consists of two dimensions: self-assertion and separateness.

Social influence Social influence is when the actions or thoughts of individual(s) are changed by other individual(s). Peer pressure is an example of social influence.

Heredity Heredity is the transfer of characteristics from parent to offspring through their genes.

Socialization Social rules and social relations are created, communicated, and changed in verbal and nonverbal ways creating social complexity useful in identifying outsiders and intelligent breeding partners. The process of learning these skills is called socialization.

Predisposition Predisposition refers to an inclination or diathesis to respond in a certain way, either inborn or acquired. In abnormal psychology, it is a factor that lowers the ability to

Go to **Cram101.com** for the Practice Tests for this Chapter.

withstand stress and inclines the individual toward pathology.

Go to **Cram101.com** for the Practice Tests for this Chapter.

Infatuation	The term "infatuation" carries connotations of immaturity or fatuousness, while "limerence" is intended to separate these connotations from the emotion.
Existential psychology	Existential psychology is partly based on the belief that human beings are alone in the world. This aloneness leads to feelings of meaninglessness which can be overcome only by creating one's own values and meanings
Kierkegaard	Kierkegaard has achieved general recognition as the first existentialist philosopher, though some new research shows this may be a more difficult connection than previously thought.
Nietzsche	Nietzsche in his own estimation was a psychologist. His works helped to reinforce not only agnostic trends that followed Enlightenment thinkers, and the evolutionary theory of Charles Darwin, but also the interpretations of human behavior by Sigmund Freud.
Heidegger	Heidegger is regarded as a major influence on existentialism. He focused on the phenomenon of intentionality. Human behavior is intentional insofar as it is directed at some object or end (all building is building of something, all talking is talking about something, etc).
Scientific research	Research that is objective, systematic, and testable is called scientific research.
Insight	Insight refers to a sudden awareness of the relationships among various elements that had previously appeared to be independent of one another.
Rollo May	Rollo May was the best known American existential psychologist, authoring the influential book Love and Will in 1969. He differs from other humanistic psychologists in showing a sharper awareness of the tragic dimensions of human existence.
Erik Erikson	Erik Erikson conceived eight stages of development, each confronting the individual with its own psychosocial demands, that continued into old age. Personality development, according to Erikson, takes place through a series of crises that must be overcome and internalized by the individual in preparation for the next developmental stage. Such crisis are not catastrophes but vulnerabilities.
Carl Rogers	Carl Rogers was instrumental in the development of non-directive psychotherapy, also known as "client-centered" psychotherapy. Rogers' basic tenets were unconditional positive regard, genuineness, and empathic understanding, with each demonstrated by the counselor.
Adler	Adler argued that human personality could be explained teleologically, separate strands dominated by the guiding purpose of the individual's unconscious self ideal to convert feelings of inferiority to superiority (or rather completeness). The desires of the self ideal were countered by social and ethical demands.
Sullivan	Sullivan developed the Self System, a configuration of the personality traits developed in childhood and reinforced by positive affirmation and the security operations developed in childhood to avoid anxiety and threats to self-esteem.
Clinical psychology	Clinical psychology is involved in the diagnosis, assessment, and treatment of patients with mental or behavioral disorders, and conducts research in these various areas.
Psychotherapy	Psychotherapy is a set of techniques based on psychological principles intended to improve mental health, emotional or behavioral issues. Commonly psychotherapy involves a therapist and client(s), who discuss their issues in an effort to discover what they are and how they can solve them.
Anxiety	Anxiety is a complex combination of the feeling of fear, apprehension and worry often accompanied by physical sensations such as palpitations, chest pain and/or shortness of breath.
Society	The social sciences use the term society to mean a group of people that form a semi-closed

Go to **Cram101.com** for the Practice Tests for this Chapter.

Go to **Cram101.com** for the Practice Tests for this Chapter.
And, **NEVER** highlight a book again!

	(or semi-open) social system, in which most interactions are with other individuals belonging to the group.
Clinical psychologist	A psychologist, usually with a Ph.D, whose training is in the diagnosis, treatment, or research of psychological and behavioral disorders is a clinical psychologist.
Existentialism	The view that people are completely free and responsible for their own behavior is existentialism.
Dehumanization	Dehumanization is a process by which members of a group of people assert the "inferiority" of another group through subtle or overt acts or statements.
Dichotomy	A dichotomy is the division of a proposition into two parts which are both mutually exclusive – i.e. both cannot be simultaneously true – and jointly exhaustive – i.e. they cover the full range of possible outcomes. They are often contrasting and spoken of as "opposites".
Emotion	An emotion is a mental states that arise spontaneously, rather than through conscious effort. They are often accompanied by physiological changes.
Attention	Attention is the cognitive process of selectively concentrating on one thing while ignoring other things. Psychologists have labeled three types of attention: sustained attention, selective attention, and divided attention.
Acquisition	Acquisition is the process of adapting to the environment, learning or becoming conditioned. In classical conditoning terms, it is the initial learning of the stimulus response link, which involves a neutral stimulus being associated with a unconditioned stimulus and becoming a conditioned stimulus.
Psychiatrist	A psychiatrist is a physician who specializes in the diagnosis and treatment of psychological disorders.
Binswanger	Binswanger is considered the founder of existential psychology. In the early 1920s he turned increasingly towards an existential rather than Freudian perspective, so that by the early 1930s he had become the first existential therapist.
Theories	Theories are logically self-consistent models or frameworks describing the behavior of a certain natural or social phenomenon. They are broad explanations and predictions concerning phenomena of interest.
Phenomenological approach	The assumption that one must appreciate individuals' personal, subjective experiences to truly understand their behavior is a phenomenological approach.
Instinct	Instinct is the word used to describe inherent dispositions towards particular actions. They are generally an inherited pattern of responses or reactions to certain kinds of situations.
Personality	Personality refers to the pattern of enduring characteristics that differentiates a person, the patterns of behaviors that make each individual unique.
Psychopathology	Psychopathology refers to the field concerned with the nature and development of mental disorders.
Intentionality	Brentano defined intentionality as the main characteristic of "psychical phenomena," by which they could be distinguished from "physical phenomena.". Every mental phenomenon, every psychological act has a content, is directed at an object (the intentional object).
Neurotic anxiety	Neurotic anxiety refers to, in psychoanalytic theory, a fear of the consequences of expressing previously punished and repressed id impulses; more generally, unrealistic fear.
Repression	A defense mechanism, repression involves moving thoughts unacceptable to the ego into the unconscious, where they cannot be easily accessed.
Infancy	The developmental period that extends from birth to 18 or 24 months is called infancy.

Go to **Cram101.com** for the Practice Tests for this Chapter.

Go to **Cram101.com** for the Practice Tests for this Chapter.
And, **NEVER** highlight a book again!

Intrapsychic conflict	In psychoanalysis, the struggles among the id, ego, and superego are an intrapsychic conflict.
Blocking	If the one of the two members of a compound stimulus fails to produce the CR due to an earlier conditioning of the other member of the compound stimulus, blocking has occurred.
Learning	Learning is a relatively permanent change in behavior that results from experience. Thus, to attribute a behavioral change to learning, the change must be relatively permanent and must result from experience.
Early childhood	Early childhood refers to the developmental period extending from the end of infancy to about 5 or 6 years of age; sometimes called the preschool years.
Attachment	Attachment is the tendency to seek closeness to another person and feel secure when that person is present.
Guilt	Guilt describes many concepts related to a negative emotion or condition caused by actions which are believed to be, morally wrong. According to Freud, the avoidance of guilt is the basis for moral behavior.
Individuality	According to Cooper, individuality consists of two dimensions: self-assertion and separateness.
Denial	Denial is a psychological defense mechanism in which a person faced with a fact that is uncomfortable or painful to accept rejects it instead, insisting that it is not true despite what may be overwhelming evidence.
Depression	In everyday language depression refers to any downturn in mood, which may be relatively transitory and perhaps due to something trivial. This is differentiated from Clinical depression which is marked by symptoms that last two weeks or more and are so severe that they interfere with daily living.
Apathy	Apathy is the lack of emotion, motivation, or enthusiasm. Apathy is a psychological term for a state of indifference — where an individual is unresponsive or "indifferent" to aspects of emotional, social, or physical life. Clinical apathy is considered to be at an elevated level, while a moderate level might be considered depression, and an extreme level could be diagnosed as a dissociative disorder.
Arousal	Arousal is a physiological and psychological state involving the activation of the reticular activating system in the brain stem, the autonomic nervous system and the endocrine system, leading to increased heart rate and blood pressure and a condition of alertness and readiness to respond.
Eros	In Freudian psychology, Eros is the life instinct innate in all humans. It is the desire to create life and favours productivity and construction. Eros battles against the destructive death instinct of Thanatos.
Species	Species refers to a reproductively isolated breeding population.
Friendship	The essentials of friendship are reciprocity and commitment between individuals who see themselves more or less as equals. Interaction between friends rests on a more equal power base than the interaction between children and adults.
Late adolescence	Late adolescence refers to approximately the latter half of the second decade of life. Career interests, dating, and identity exploration are often more pronounced in late adolescence than in early adolescence.
Adolescence	The period of life bounded by puberty and the assumption of adult responsibilities is adolescence.
Predisposition	Predisposition refers to an inclination or diathesis to respond in a certain way, either

Go to **Cram101.com** for the Practice Tests for this Chapter.

inborn or acquired. In abnormal psychology, it is a factor that lowers the ability to withstand stress and inclines the individual toward pathology.

Attitude	An enduring mental representation of a person, place, or thing that evokes an emotional response and related behavior is called attitude.
Perception	Perception is the process of acquiring, interpreting, selecting, and organizing sensory information.
Drug addiction	Drug addiction, or substance dependence is the compulsive use of drugs, to the point where the user has no effective choice but to continue use.
Addiction	Addiction is an uncontrollable compulsion to repeat a behavior regardless of its consequences. Many drugs or behaviors can precipitate a pattern of conditions recognized as addiction, which include a craving for more of the drug or behavior, increased physiological tolerance to exposure, and withdrawal symptoms in the absence of the stimulus.
Meditation	Meditation usually refers to a state in which the body is consciously relaxed and the mind is allowed to become calm and focused.
Incest	Incest refers to sexual relations between close relatives, most often between daughter and father or between brother and sister.
Collective unconscious	Collective unconscious is a term of analytical psychology, originally coined by Carl Jung. It refers to that part of a person's unconscious which is common to all human beings. It contains archetypes, which are forms or symbols that are manifested by all people in all cultures.
Archetype	The archetype is a concept of psychologist Carl Jung. They are innate prototypes for ideas, which may subsequently become involved in the interpretation of observed phenomena. A group of memories and interpretations closely associated with an archetype is called a complex.
Empathy	Empathy is the recognition and understanding of the states of mind, including beliefs, desires and particularly emotions of others without injecting your own.
Questionnaire	A self-report method of data collection or clinical assessment method in which the individual being studied checks off items on a printed list, answers multiple-choice questions, or writes out answers to essay questions aimed at producing a selfdescription is called questionnaire.
Empirical	Empirical means the use of working hypotheses which are capable of being disproved using observation or experiment.
Otto Rank	Otto Rank extended psychoanalytic theory to the study of legend, myth, art, and other works of creativity. He favored a more egalitarian relationship with patients and is sometimes considered the forerunner of client-centered therapy.
Personality psychology	Personality psychology is a branch of psychology which studies personality and individual difference processes. One emphasis in personality psychology is on trying to create a coherent picture of a person and all his or her major psychological processes.
Norms	In testing, standards of test performance that permit the comparison of one person's score on the test to the scores of others who have taken the same test are referred to as norms.
Social norm	A social norm, is a rule that is socially enforced. In social situations, such as meetings, they are unwritten and often unstated rules that govern individuals' behavior. A social norm is most evident when not followed or broken.
Variable	A variable refers to a measurable factor, characteristic, or attribute of an individual or a system.

Go to **Cram101.com** for the Practice Tests for this Chapter.

Independent variable	A condition in a scientific study that is manipulated (assigned different values by a researcher) so that the effects of the manipulation may be observed is called an independent variable.
Hypothesis	A specific statement about behavior or mental processes that is testable through research is a hypothesis.
Sympathetic	The sympathetic nervous system activates what is often termed the "fight or flight response". It is an automatic regulation system, that is, one that operates without the intervention of conscious thought.
Human nature	Human nature is the fundamental nature and substance of humans, as well as the range of human behavior that is believed to be invariant over long periods of time and across very different cultural contexts.
Humanistic	Humanistic refers to any system of thought focused on subjective experience and human problems and potentials.
Distal	Students can set both long-term (distal) and short-term (proximal) goals .
Reasoning	Reasoning is the act of using reason to derive a conclusion from certain premises. There are two main methods to reach a conclusion,deductive reasoning and inductive reasoning.
Affect	A subjective feeling or emotional tone often accompanied by bodily expressions noticeable to others is called affect.
Factor analysis	Factor analysis is a statistical technique that originated in psychometrics. The objective is to explain the most of the variability among a number of observable random variables in terms of a smaller number of unobservable random variables called factors.
Operational definition	An operational definition is the definition of a concept or action in terms of the observable and repeatable process, procedures, and appartaus that illustrates the concept or action.
Parsimony	In science, parsimony is preference for the least complicated explanation for an observation. This is generally regarded as good when judging hypotheses. Occam's Razor also states the "principle of parsimony".
Consciousness	The awareness of the sensations, thoughts, and feelings being experienced at a given moment is called consciousness.
Free choice	Free choice refers to the ability to freely make choices that are not controlled by genetics, learning, or unconscious forces.
Determinism	Determinism is the philosophical proposition that every event, including human cognition and action, is causally determined by an unbroken chain of prior occurrences.
Teleology	While science investigates natural laws and phenomena, Philosophical naturalism and teleology investigate the existence or non-existence of an organizing principle behind those natural laws and phenonema. Philosophical naturalism asserts that there are no such principles. Teleology asserts that there are.
Causation	Causation concerns the time order relationship between two or more objects such that if a specific antecendent condition occurs the same consequent must always follow.
Neurosis	Neurosis, any mental disorder that, although may cause distress, does not interfere with rational thought or the persons' ability to function.
Shaping	The concept of reinforcing successive, increasingly accurate approximations to a target behavior is called shaping. The target behavior is broken down into a hierarchy of elemental steps, each step more sophisticated then the last. By successively reinforcing each of the the elemental steps, a form of differential reinforcement, until that step is learned while

Go to **Cram101.com** for the Practice Tests for this Chapter.

extinguishing the step below, the target behavior is gradually achieved.

Phenomenology	Phenomenology is the study of subjective mental experiences; a theme of humanistic theories of personality. It studies meaningful, intact mental events without dividing them for further analysis.

Sigmund Freud	Sigmund Freud was the founder of the psychoanalytic school, based on his theory that unconscious motives control much behavior, that particular kinds of unconscious thoughts and memories are the source of neurosis, and that neurosis could be treated through bringing these unconscious thoughts and memories to consciousness in psychoanalytic treatment.
Psychiatrist	A psychiatrist is a physician who specializes in the diagnosis and treatment of psychological disorders.
Phobia	A persistent, irrational fear of an object, situation, or activity that the person feels compelled to avoid is referred to as a phobia.
Personality	Personality refers to the pattern of enduring characteristics that differentiates a person, the patterns of behaviors that make each individual unique.
Allport	Allport was a trait theorist. Those traits he believed to predominate a person's personality were called central traits. Traits such that one could be indentifed by the trait, were referred to as cardinal traits. Central traits and cardinal traits are influenced by environmental factors.
Theories	Theories are logically self-consistent models or frameworks describing the behavior of a certain natural or social phenomenon. They are broad explanations and predictions concerning phenomena of interest.
Psychoanalysis	Psychoanalysis refers to the school of psychology that emphasizes the importance of unconscious motives and conflicts as determinants of human behavior. It was Freud's method of exploring human personality.
Learning	Learning is a relatively permanent change in behavior that results from experience. Thus, to attribute a behavioral change to learning, the change must be relatively permanent and must result from experience.
Humanistic	Humanistic refers to any system of thought focused on subjective experience and human problems and potentials.
Nomothetic	Nomothetic measures are contrasted to ipsative or idiothetic measures, where nomothetic measures are measures that can be taken directly by an outside observer, such as weight or how many times a particular behavior occurs, and ipsative measures are self-reports such as a rank-ordered list of preferences.
Human nature	Human nature is the fundamental nature and substance of humans, as well as the range of human behavior that is believed to be invariant over long periods of time and across very different cultural contexts.
Clinical psychology	Clinical psychology is involved in the diagnosis, assessment, and treatment of patients with mental or behavioral disorders, and conducts research in these various areas.
American Psychological Association	The American Psychological Association is a professional organization representing psychology in the US. The mission statement is to "advance psychology as a science and profession and as a means of promoting health, education , and human welfare".
Motivation	In psychology, motivation is the driving force (desire) behind all actions of an organism.
Maslow	Maslow is mostly noted today for his proposal of a hierarchy of human needs which he often presented as a pyramid. Maslow was an instrumental player in the formation of the humanistic movement, also known as the third force in psychology.
Motives	Needs or desires that energize and direct behavior toward a goal are motives.
Trauma	Trauma refers to a severe physical injury or wound to the body caused by an external force, or a psychological shock having a lasting effect on mental life.

Go to **Cram101.com** for the Practice Tests for this Chapter.

Attitude	An enduring mental representation of a person, place, or thing that evokes an emotional response and related behavior is called attitude.
Insight	Insight refers to a sudden awareness of the relationships among various elements that had previously appeared to be independent of one another.
Prejudice	Prejudice in general, implies coming to a judgment on the subject before learning where the preponderance of the evidence actually lies, or formation of a judgement without direct experience.
Instinct	Instinct is the word used to describe inherent dispositions towards particular actions. They are generally an inherited pattern of responses or reactions to certain kinds of situations.
Trait	An enduring personality characteristic that tends to lead to certain behaviors is called a trait. The term trait also means a genetically inherited feature of an organism.
Individual traits	Personality traits that define a person's unique individual qualities are called individual traits.
Common traits	Common traits, according to Allport, are personality characteristics that are shared by most members of a particular culture or grouping.
Sadism	Sadism is the sexual pleasure or gratification in the infliction of pain and suffering upon another person. It is considered to be a paraphilia. The word is derived from the name of the Marquis de Sade, a prolific French writer of sadistic novels.
Expressive behaviors	Behaviors that express or communicate emotion or personal feelings are expressive behaviors.
Functional autonomy	By functional autonomy, Allport meant that your motives today are not dependent on the past. He differentiated between perseverative functional autonomy, which refers to habits, and propriate functional autonomy which is more self-directed than habits and includes values.
Autonomy	Autonomy is the condition of something that does not depend on anything else.
Stimulus	A change in an environmental condition that elicits a response is a stimulus.
Pleasure principle	The pleasure principle is the tendency to seek pleasure and avoid pain. In Freud's theory, this principle rules the Id, but is at least partly repressed by the reality principle.
Hypothesis	A specific statement about behavior or mental processes that is testable through research is a hypothesis.
Drive reduction	Drive reduction theories are based on the need-state. Drive activates behavior. Reinforcement occurs whenever drive is reduced, leading to learning of whatever response solves the need. Thus the reduction in need serves as reinforcement and produces reinforcement of the response that leads to it.
Contemporaneity	The belief that only present facts can or should influence present thinking and behavior is the principle of contemporaneity.
Adler	Adler argued that human personality could be explained teleologically, separate strands dominated by the guiding purpose of the individual's unconscious self ideal to convert feelings of inferiority to superiority (or rather completeness). The desires of the self ideal were countered by social and ethical demands.
Anatomy	Anatomy is the branch of biology that deals with the structure and organization of living things. It can be divided into animal anatomy (zootomy) and plant anatomy (phytonomy). Major branches of anatomy include comparative anatomy, histology, and human anatomy.
Primary drive	A primary drive is a state of tension or arousal arising from a biological or innate need; it is one not based on learning. A primary drive activates behavior.

Go to **Cram101.com** for the Practice Tests for this Chapter.

Alcoholic	An alcoholic is dependent on alcohol as characterized by craving, loss of control, physical dependence and withdrawal symptoms, and tolerance.
Reflex	A simple, involuntary response to a stimulus is referred to as reflex. Reflex actions originate at the spinal cord rather than the brain.
Temperament	Temperament refers to a basic, innate disposition to change behavior. The activity level is an important dimension of temperament.
Reinforcement	In operant conditioning, reinforcement is any change in an environment that (a) occurs after the behavior, (b) seems to make that behavior re-occur more often in the future and (c) that reoccurence of behavior must be the result of the change.
Sublimation	Sublimation is a coping mechanism. It refers to rechanneling sexual or aggressive energy into pursuits that society considers acceptable or admirable.
Primary reinforcement	The use of reinforcers that are innately or biologically satisfying is called primary reinforcement.
Habit	A habit is a response that has become completely separated from its eliciting stimulus. Early learning theorists used the term to describe S-R associations, however not all S-R associations become a habit, rather many are extinguished after reinforcement is withdrawn.
Compulsion	An apparently irresistible urge to repeat an act or engage in ritualistic behavior such as hand washing is referred to as a compulsion.
Neurosis	Neurosis, any mental disorder that, although may cause distress, does not interfere with rational thought or the persons' ability to function.
Research method	The scope of the research method is to produce some new knowledge. This, in principle, can take three main forms: Exploratory research; Constructive research; and Empirical research.
Idiographic	An idiographic investigation studies the characteristics of an individual in depth.
Hans Eysenck	Hans Eysenck using Factor Analysis concluded that all human traits can be broken down into two distinct categories: 1. Extroversion-Introversion, 2. Neuroticism. He called these categories Supertraits.
Validity	The extent to which a test measures what it is intended to measure is called validity.
Psychological test	Psychological test refers to a standardized measure of a sample of a person's behavior.
Unconscious mind	The unconscious mind refers to information processing and brain functioning of which a person is unaware. In Freudian theory,it is the repository of unacceptable thoughts and feelings.
Psychoanalyst	A psychoanalyst is a specially trained therapist who attempts to treat the individual by uncovering and revealing to the individual otherwise subconscious factors that are contributing to some undesirable behavior.
Need for Affiliation	Need for Affiliation is a term introduced by David McClelland to describe a person's need to feel like he needs to belong to a group. These individuals require warm interpersonal relationships and approval from those in these relationships is very satisfying. People who value affiliation a lot tend to be good team members, but poor leaders.
Psychometric	Psychometric study is concerned with the theory and technique of psychological measurement, which includes the measurement of knowledge, abilities, attitudes, and personality traits. The field is primarily concerned with the study of differences between individuals
Depression	In everyday language depression refers to any downturn in mood, which may be relatively transitory and perhaps due to something trivial. This is differentiated from Clinical depression which is marked by symptoms that last two weeks or more and are so severe that

Go to **Cram101.com** for the Practice Tests for this Chapter.

they interfere with daily living.

Dichotomy	A dichotomy is the division of a proposition into two parts which are both mutually exclusive – i.e. both cannot be simultaneously true – and jointly exhaustive – i.e. they cover the full range of possible outcomes. They are often contrasting and spoken of as "opposites".
Stroke	A stroke occurs when the blood supply to a part of the brain is suddenly interrupted by occlusion, by hemorrhage, or other causes
Hypertension	Hypertension is a medical condition where the blood pressure in the arteries is chronically elevated. Persistent hypertension is one of the risk factors for strokes, heart attacks, heart failure and arterial aneurysm, and is a leading cause of chronic renal failure.
Social support	Social Support is the physical and emotional comfort given by family, friends, co-workers and others. Research has identified three main types of social support: emotional, practical, sharing points of view.
Falsifiability	According to Popper the extent to which a scientific assertion is amenable to systematic probes, any one of which could negate the scientist's expectations is referred to as falsifiability.
Early childhood	Early childhood refers to the developmental period extending from the end of infancy to about 5 or 6 years of age; sometimes called the preschool years.
Conformity	Conformity is the degree to which members of a group will change their behavior, views and attitudes to fit the views of the group. The group can influence members via unconscious processes or via overt social pressure on individuals.
Society	The social sciences use the term society to mean a group of people that form a semi-closed (or semi-open) social system, in which most interactions are with other individuals belonging to the group.
Shaping	The concept of reinforcing successive, increasingly accurate approximations to a target behavior is called shaping. The target behavior is broken down into a hierarchy of elemental steps, each step more sophisticated then the last. By successively reinforcing each of the the elemental steps, a form of differential reinforcement, until that step is learned while extinguishing the step below, the target behavior is gradually achieved.
Heredity	Heredity is the transfer of characteristics from parent to offspring through their genes.
Free will	The idea that human beings are capable of freely making choices or decisions is free will.
Free choice	Free choice refers to the ability to freely make choices that are not controlled by genetics, learning, or unconscious forces.
Consciousness	The awareness of the sensations, thoughts, and feelings being experienced at a given moment is called consciousness.
Individual differences	Individual differences psychology studies the ways in which individual people differ in their behavior. This is distinguished from other aspects of psychology in that although psychology is ostensibly a study of individuals, modern psychologists invariably study groups.
Perception	Perception is the process of acquiring, interpreting, selecting, and organizing sensory information.

Go to **Cram101.com** for the Practice Tests for this Chapter.

Psychoanalysis	Psychoanalysis refers to the school of psychology that emphasizes the importance of unconscious motives and conflicts as determinants of human behavior. It was Freud's method of exploring human personality.
Trait	An enduring personality characteristic that tends to lead to certain behaviors is called a trait. The term trait also means a genetically inherited feature of an organism.
Personality	Personality refers to the pattern of enduring characteristics that differentiates a person, the patterns of behaviors that make each individual unique.
Personality trait	According to the Diagnostic and Statistical Manual of the American Psychiatric Association, a personality trait is a "prominent aspect of personality that is exhibited in a wide range of important social and personal contexts. ...".
Theories	Theories are logically self-consistent models or frameworks describing the behavior of a certain natural or social phenomenon. They are broad explanations and predictions concerning phenomena of interest.
Openness to Experience	Openness to Experience, one of the big-five traits, describes a dimension of cognitive style that distinguishes imaginative, creative people from down-to-earth, conventional people.
Neuroticism	Eysenck's use of the term neuroticism (or Emotional Stability) was proposed as the dimension describing individual differences in the predisposition towards neurotic disorder.
Extraversion	Extraversion, one of the big-five personailty traits, is marked by pronounced engagement with the external world. They are people who enjoy being with people, are full of energy, and often experience positive emotions.
Big five	The big five factors of personality are Openness to experience, Conscientiousness, Extraversion, Agreeableness, and Emotional Stability.
Conscientiou-ness	Conscientiousness is one of the dimensions of the five-factor model of personality and individual differences involving being organized, thorough, and reliable as opposed to careless, negligent, and unreliable.
Agreeableness	Agreeableness, one of the big-five personality traits, reflects individual differences in concern with cooperation and social harmony. It is the degree individuals value getting along with others.
Attitude	An enduring mental representation of a person, place, or thing that evokes an emotional response and related behavior is called attitude.
Deprivation	Deprivation, is the loss or withholding of normal stimulation, nutrition, comfort, love, and so forth; a condition of lacking. The level of stimulation is less than what is required.
Psychometric	Psychometric study is concerned with the theory and technique of psychological measurement, which includes the measurement of knowledge, abilities, attitudes, and personality traits. The field is primarily concerned with the study of differences between individuals
Cyril Burt	Cyril Burt was controversial for his conclusions that genetics substantially influence mental and behavioral traits.
Charles Spearman	Charles Spearman is known for his work in statistics, as a pioneer of factor analysis, and for his rank correlation coefficient. He also did seminal work on models for human intelligence, including discovering that disparate cognitive test scores reflect a single general factor and coining the term g factor.
Factor analysis	Factor analysis is a statistical technique that originated in psychometrics. The objective is to explain the most of the variability among a number of observable random variables in terms of a smaller number of unobservable random variables called factors.

Go to **Cram101.com** for the Practice Tests for this Chapter.

Clinical psychology	Clinical psychology is involved in the diagnosis, assessment, and treatment of patients with mental or behavioral disorders, and conducts research in these various areas.
Neurosis	Neurosis, any mental disorder that, although may cause distress, does not interfere with rational thought or the persons' ability to function.
Creativity	Creativity is the ability to think about something in novel and unusual ways and come up with unique solutions to problems. It involves divergent thinking, having many solutions or views to a problem.
Placebo	Placebo refers to a bogus treatment that has the appearance of being genuine.
Arthur Jensen	Arthur Jensen was a major practitioner of individual differences psychology with a special interest in intelligence and the nature versus nurture debate, and argued strongly that intelligence is partially heritable.
Individual differences	Individual differences psychology studies the ways in which individual people differ in their behavior. This is distinguished from other aspects of psychology in that although psychology is ostensibly a study of individuals, modern psychologists invariably study groups.
Society	The social sciences use the term society to mean a group of people that form a semi-closed (or semi-open) social system, in which most interactions are with other individuals belonging to the group.
Trait theory	According to trait theory, personality can be broken down into a limited number of traits, which are present in each individual to a greater or lesser degree. This approach is highly compatible with the quantitative psychometric approach to personality testing.
Reasoning	Reasoning is the act of using reason to derive a conclusion from certain premises. There are two main methods to reach a conclusion,deductive reasoning and inductive reasoning.
Deductive reasoning	Deductive reasoning refers to a form of reasoning about arguments in which conclusions are determined from the premises. The conclusions are true if the premises are true.
Questionnaire	A self-report method of data collection or clinical assessment method in which the individual being studied checks off items on a printed list, answers multiple-choice questions, or writes out answers to essay questions aimed at producing a selfdescription is called questionnaire.
Temperament	Temperament refers to a basic, innate disposition to change behavior. The activity level is an important dimension of temperament.
Motivation	In psychology, motivation is the driving force (desire) behind all actions of an organism.
Population	Population refers to all members of a well-defined group of organisms, events, or things.
Eysenck Personality Questionnaire	The Eysenck Personality Questionnaire measures the three traits described in the personality theory of Hans Eysenck. These are extraversion, psychoticism, and neuroticism.
Variable	A variable refers to a measurable factor, characteristic, or attribute of an individual or a system.
Correlation	A statistical technique for determining the degree of association between two or more variables is referred to as correlation.
Correlation coefficient	Correlation coefficient refers to a number from +1.00 to -1.00 that expresses the direction and extent of the relationship between two variables. The closer to 1, the stronger the relationship. The sign, + or -, indicates the direction.
Heritability	Heritability It is that proportion of the observed variation in a particular phenotype within a particular population, that can be attributed to the contribution of genotype. In other

Go to Cram101.com for the Practice Tests for this Chapter.

words: it measures the extent to which differences between individuals in a population are due their being different genetically.

Psychotic behavior	A psychotic behavior is a severe psychological disorder characterized by hallucinations and loss of contact with reality.
Drug addiction	Drug addiction, or substance dependence is the compulsive use of drugs, to the point where the user has no effective choice but to continue use.
Addiction	Addiction is an uncontrollable compulsion to repeat a behavior regardless of its consequences. Many drugs or behaviors can precipitate a pattern of conditions recognized as addiction, which include a craving for more of the drug or behavior, increased physiological tolerance to exposure, and withdrawal symptoms in the absence of the stimulus.
Cognition	The intellectual processes through which information is obtained, transformed, stored, retrieved, and otherwise used is cognition.
Habit	A habit is a response that has become completely separated from its eliciting stimulus. Early learning theorists used the term to describe S-R associations, however not all S-R associations become a habit, rather many are extinguished after reinforcement is withdrawn.
Shyness	A tendency to avoid others plus uneasiness and strain when socializing is called shyness.
Introversion	A personality trait characterized by intense imagination and a tendency to inhibit impulses is called introversion.
Source traits	Cattell's name for the traits that make up the most basic personality structure and causes of behavior is source traits.
Psychoticism	Psychoticism is one of the three traits used by the psychologist Hans Eysenck in his P-E-N model of personality. High levels of this trait were believed by Eysenck to be linked to increased vulnerability to psychoses such as schizophrenia.
Shaping	The concept of reinforcing successive, increasingly accurate approximations to a target behavior is called shaping. The target behavior is broken down into a hierarchy of elemental steps, each step more sophisticated then the last. By successively reinforcing each of the the elemental steps, a form of differential reinforcement, until that step is learned while extinguishing the step below, the target behavior is gradually achieved.
Sigmund Freud	Sigmund Freud was the founder of the psychoanalytic school, based on his theory that unconscious motives control much behavior, that particular kinds of unconscious thoughts and memories are the source of neurosis, and that neurosis could be treated through bringing these unconscious thoughts and memories to consciousness in psychoanalytic treatment.
Jung	Jung was in some aspects a response to Sigmund Freud's psychoanalysis. He proposed and developed the concepts of the extroverted and introverted personality, archetypes, and the collective unconscious. His work has been influential in psychiatry and in the study of religion, literature, and related fields.
Anxiety	Anxiety is a complex combination of the feeling of fear, apprehension and worry often accompanied by physical sensations such as palpitations, chest pain and/or shortness of breath.
Introvert	Introvert refers to a person whose attention is focused inward; a shy, reserved, timid person.
Arousal	Arousal is a physiological and psychological state involving the activation of the reticular activating system in the brain stem, the autonomic nervous system and the endocrine system, leading to increased heart rate and blood pressure and a condition of alertness and readiness to respond.

Threshold	In general, a threshold is a fixed location or value where an abrupt change is observed. In the sensory modalities, it is the minimum amount of stimulus energy necessary to elicit a sensory response.
Hysteria	Hysteria is a diagnostic label applied to a state of mind, one of unmanageable fear or emotional excesses. The fear is often centered on a body part, most often on an imagined problem with that body part.
Fraternal twins	Fraternal twins usually occur when two fertilized eggs are implanted in the uterine wall at the same time. The two eggs form two zygotes, and these twins are therefore also known as dizygotic. Dizygotic twins are no more similar genetically than any siblings.
Homosexuality	Homosexuality refers to a sexual orientation characterized by aesthetic attraction, romantic love, and sexual desire exclusively for members of the same sex or gender identity.
Identical twins	Identical twins occur when a single egg is fertilized to form one zygote (monozygotic) but the zygote then divides into two separate embryos. The two embryos develop into foetuses sharing the same womb. Monozygotic twins are genetically identical unless there has been a mutation in development, and they are almost always the same gender.
Alcoholism	A disorder that involves long-term, repeated, uncontrolled, compulsive, and excessive use of alcoholic beverages and that impairs the drinker's health and work and social relationships is called alcoholism.
Diathesis	A predisposition toward a disease or abnormality is a diathesis.
Syndrome	The term syndrome is the association of several clinically recognizable features, signs, symptoms, phenomena or characteristics which often occur together, so that the presence of one feature indicates the presence of the others.
Superego	Frued's third psychic structure, which functions as a moral guardian and sets forth high standards for behavior is the superego.
Egocentrism	The inability to distinguish between one's own perspective and someone else's is referred to as egocentrism.
Psychological disorder	Mental processes and/or behavior patterns that cause emotional distress and/or substantial impairment in functioning is a psychological disorder.
Scheme	According to Piaget, a hypothetical mental structure that permits the classification and organization of new information is called a scheme.
Personality inventory	A self-report questionnaire by which an examinee indicates whether statements assessing habitual tendencies apply to him or her is referred to as a personality inventory.
Antecedents	In behavior modification, events that typically precede the target response are called antecedents.
Conditioning	Conditioning describes the process by which behaviors can be learned or modified through interaction with the environment.
Psychopathology	Psychopathology refers to the field concerned with the nature and development of mental disorders.
Proximal	Students can set both long-term (distal) and short-term (proximal) goals .
Laboratory study	Any research study in which the subjects are brought to a specially designated area that has been set up to facilitate the researcher's ability to control the environment or collect data is referred to as a laboratory study.
Distal	Students can set both long-term (distal) and short-term (proximal) goals .

Go to **Cram101.com** for the Practice Tests for this Chapter.

Attention	Attention is the cognitive process of selectively concentrating on one thing while ignoring other things. Psychologists have labeled three types of attention: sustained attention, selective attention, and divided attention.
Behavior therapy	Behavior therapy refers to the systematic application of the principles of learning to direct modification of a client's problem behaviors.
Autonomy	Autonomy is the condition of something that does not depend on anything else.
Raymond Cattell	Raymond Cattell proposed that 16 factors underlie human personality. He called these 16 factors source traits because he believed that they provide the underlying source for the surface behaviors that we think of as personality.
Clinical psychologist	A psychologist, usually with a Ph.D, whose training is in the diagnosis, treatment, or research of psychological and behavioral disorders is a clinical psychologist.
Mischel	Mischel is known for his cognitive social learning model of personality that focuses on the specific cognitive variables that mediate the manner in which new experiences affect the individual.
Response set	A tendency to answer test items according to a personal or situational bias is called response set.
Stereotype	A stereotype is considered to be a group concept, held by one social group about another. They are often used in a negative or prejudicial sense and are frequently used to justify certain discriminatory behaviors. This allows powerful social groups to legitimize and protect their dominant position
Gerontology	Gerontology is the study of the elderly, and of the aging process itself. It is to be distinguished from geriatrics, which is the study of the diseases of the elderly. Gerontology covers the social, psychological and biology aspects of aging.
Humanistic	Humanistic refers to any system of thought focused on subjective experience and human problems and potentials.
American Psychological Association	The American Psychological Association is a professional organization representing psychology in the US. The mission statement is to "advance psychology as a science and profession and as a means of promoting health, education , and human welfare".
Allport	Allport was a trait theorist. Those traits he believed to predominate a person's personality were called central traits. Traits such that one could be indentifed by the trait, were referred to as cardinal traits. Central traits and cardinal traits are influenced by environmental factors.
Evolution	Commonly used to refer to gradual change, evolution is the change in the frequency of alleles within a population from one generation to the next. This change may be caused by different mechanisms, including natural selection, genetic drift, or changes in population (gene flow).
Insight	Insight refers to a sudden awareness of the relationships among various elements that had previously appeared to be independent of one another.
Empirical	Empirical means the use of working hypotheses which are capable of being disproved using observation or experiment.
Adaptation	Adaptation is a lowering of sensitivity to a stimulus following prolonged exposure to that stimulus. Behavioral adaptations are special ways a particular organism behaves to survive in its natural habitat.
Adaption	Adaption is a lowering of sensitive to a stimulus following prolonged exposure to that stimulus. Behavioral adaptations are special ways a particular organism behaves to survive in its natural habitat.

Go to **Cram101.com** for the Practice Tests for this Chapter.

Sexual orientation	Sexual orientation refers to the sex or gender of people who are the focus of a person's amorous or erotic desires, fantasies, and spontaneous feelings, the gender(s) toward which one is primarily "oriented".
Acquisition	Acquisition is the process of adapting to the environment, learning or becoming conditioned. In classical conditoning terms, it is the initial learning of the stimulus response link, which involves a neutral stimulus being associated with a unconditioned stimulus and becoming a conditioned stimulus.
Statistic	A statistic is an observable random variable of a sample.
Statistics	Statistics is a type of data analysis which practice includes the planning, summarizing, and interpreting of observations of a system possibly followed by predicting or forecasting of future events based on a mathematical model of the system being observed.
Plasticity	The capacity for modification and change is referred to as plasticity.
Learning	Learning is a relatively permanent change in behavior that results from experience. Thus, to attribute a behavioral change to learning, the change must be relatively permanent and must result from experience.
Bandura	Bandura is best known for his work on social learning theory or Social Cognitivism. His famous Bobo doll experiment illustrated that people learn from observing others.
Carl Rogers	Carl Rogers was instrumental in the development of non-directive psychotherapy, also known as "client-centered" psychotherapy. Rogers' basic tenets were unconditional positive regard, genuineness, and empathic understanding, with each demonstrated by the counselor.
Psychodynamic	Most psychodynamic approaches are centered around the idea of a maladapted function developed early in life (usually childhood) which are at least in part unconscious. This maladapted function (a.k.a. defense mechanism) does not do well in place of a normal/healthy one.
Ego	In Freud's view the Ego serves to balance our primitive needs and our moral beliefs and taboos. Relying on experience, a healthy Ego provides the ability to adapt to reality and interact with the outside world.
Gene	A gene is an ultramicroscopic area of the chromosome. It is the smallest physical unit of the DNA molecule that carries a piece of hereditary information.
Hormone	A hormone is a chemical messenger from one cell (or group of cells) to another. The best known are those produced by endocrine glands, but they are produced by nearly every organ system. The function of hormones is to serve as a signal to the target cells; the action of the hormone is determined by the pattern of secretion and the signal transduction of the receiving tissue.
Brain	The brain controls and coordinates most movement, behavior and homeostatic body functions such as heartbeat, blood pressure, fluid balance and body temperature. Functions of the brain are responsible for cognition, emotion, memory, motor learning and other sorts of learning. The brain is primarily made up of two types of cells: glia and neurons.
Genetics	Genetics is the science of genes, heredity, and the variation of organisms.
Behavioral genetics	Behavioral genetics is the field of biology that studies the role of genetics in behavior.
Brain imaging	Brain imaging is a fairly recent discipline within medicine and neuroscience. Brain imaging falls into two broad categories -- structural imaging and functional imaging.
Context	In Psychology, context refers to the background stimuli that accompany some kind of foreground event.

Go to **Cram101.com** for the Practice Tests for this Chapter.

Go to **Cram101.com** for the Practice Tests for this Chapter.
And, **NEVER** highlight a book again!

Postulates	Postulates are general statements about behavior that cannot be directly verified. They are used to generate theorems which can be tested.
Individuality	According to Cooper, individuality consists of two dimensions: self-assertion and separateness.
Variability	Statistically, variability refers to how much the scores in a distribution spread out, away from the mean.
Genotype	The genotype is the specific genetic makeup of an individual, usually in the form of DNA. It codes for the phenotype of that individual. Any given gene will usually cause an observable change in an organism, known as the phenotype.
Affect	A subjective feeling or emotional tone often accompanied by bodily expressions noticeable to others is called affect.
Hypnosis	Hypnosis is a psychological state whose existence and effects are strongly debated. Some believe that it is a state under which the subject's mind becomes so suggestible that the hypnotist, the one who induces the state, can establish communication with the subconscious mind of the subject and command behavior that the subject would not choose to perform in a conscious state.
Astrology	Astrology is any of several traditions or systems in which knowledge of the apparent positions of celestial bodies is held to be useful in understanding, interpreting, and organizing knowledge about human existence.
Abnormal psychology	The scientific study whose objectives are to describe, explain, predict, and control behaviors that are considered strange or unusual is referred to as abnormal psychology.
Species	Species refers to a reproductively isolated breeding population.
Biological model	An explanation of a psychological dysfunction that primarily emphasizes brain disorder or illness as the cause is called a biological model.
Extrovert	Extrovert refers to a person whose attention is directed outward; a bold, outgoing person.
Baseline	Measure of a particular behavior or process taken before the introduction of the independent variable or treatment is called the baseline.
Hypothesis	A specific statement about behavior or mental processes that is testable through research is a hypothesis.
Response rate	The response rate is usually calculated by dividing the total number of responses by the time available for the response.
Disinhibition	A temporary increase in the strength of an extinguished response caused by an unrelated stimulus event is referred to as disinhibition.
Depression	In everyday language depression refers to any downturn in mood, which may be relatively transitory and perhaps due to something trivial. This is differentiated from Clinical depression which is marked by symptoms that last two weeks or more and are so severe that they interfere with daily living.
Longitudinal study	Longitudinal study is a type of developmental study in which the same group of participants is followed and measured for an extended period of time, often years.
Standard deviation	In probability and statistics, the standard deviation is the most commonly used measure of statistical dispersion. Simply put, it measures how spread out the values in a data set are.
Extroversion	Extroversion refers to the tendency to be outgoing, adaptable, and sociable.
Counselor	A counselor is a mental health professional who specializes in helping people with problems

Go to **Cram101.com** for the Practice Tests for this Chapter.

not involving serious mental disorders.

Parsimony	In science, parsimony is preference for the least complicated explanation for an observation. This is generally regarded as good when judging hypotheses. Occam's Razor also states the "principle of parsimony".
Free choice	Free choice refers to the ability to freely make choices that are not controlled by genetics, learning, or unconscious forces.
Determinism	Determinism is the philosophical proposition that every event, including human cognition and action, is causally determined by an unbroken chain of prior occurrences.
Consciousness	The awareness of the sensations, thoughts, and feelings being experienced at a given moment is called consciousness.
Premise	A premise is a statement presumed true within the context of a discourse, especially of a logical argument.
Correlational study	A correlational study observes or measures two or more variables to find relationships between them. Such studies can identify lawful relationships but cannot determine whether change in one variable is the cause of change in another.
Nonconformity	Nonconformity occurs when individuals know what people around them expect but do not use those expectations to guide their behavior.
Empathy	Empathy is the recognition and understanding of the states of mind, including beliefs, desires and particularly emotions of others without injecting your own.

Identity crisis	Erikson coinded the term identity crisis: "...a psychosocial state or condition of disorientation and role confusion occurring especially in adolescents as a result of conflicting internal and external experiences, pressures, and expectations and often producing acute anxiety."
Erik Erikson	Erik Erikson conceived eight stages of development, each confronting the individual with its own psychosocial demands, that continued into old age. Personality development, according to Erikson, takes place through a series of crises that must be overcome and internalized by the individual in preparation for the next developmental stage. Such crisis are not catastrophes but vulnerabilities.
Skinner	Skinner conducted research on shaping behavior through positive and negative reinforcement, and demonstrated operant conditioning, a technique which he developed in contrast with classical conditioning.
Theories	Theories are logically self-consistent models or frameworks describing the behavior of a certain natural or social phenomenon. They are broad explanations and predictions concerning phenomena of interest.
Personality	Personality refers to the pattern of enduring characteristics that differentiates a person, the patterns of behaviors that make each individual unique.
Psychometric	Psychometric study is concerned with the theory and technique of psychological measurement, which includes the measurement of knowledge, abilities, attitudes, and personality traits. The field is primarily concerned with the study of differences between individuals
Laboratory study	Any research study in which the subjects are brought to a specially designated area that has been set up to facilitate the researcher's ability to control the environment or collect data is referred to as a laboratory study.
Jung	Jung was in some aspects a response to Sigmund Freud's psychoanalysis. He proposed and developed the concepts of the extroverted and introverted personality, archetypes, and the collective unconscious. His work has been influential in psychiatry and in the study of religion, literature, and related fields.
Behaviorism	The school of psychology that defines psychology as the study of observable behavior and studies relationships between stimuli and responses is called behaviorism. Behaviorism relied heavily on animal research and stated the same principles governed the behavior of both nonhumans and humans.
Adler	Adler argued that human personality could be explained teleologically, separate strands dominated by the guiding purpose of the individual's unconscious self ideal to convert feelings of inferiority to superiority (or rather completeness). The desires of the self ideal were countered by social and ethical demands.
Trait	An enduring personality characteristic that tends to lead to certain behaviors is called a trait. The term trait also means a genetically inherited feature of an organism.
Radical behaviorism	Skinner defined behavior to include everything that an organism does, including thinking, feeling and speaking and argued that these phenomena were valid subject matters of psychology. The term Radical Behaviorism refers to "everything an organism does is a behavior."
Ego	In Freud's view the Ego serves to balance our primitive needs and our moral beliefs and taboos. Relying on experience, a healthy Ego provides the ability to adapt to reality and interact with the outside world.
Construct	A generalized concept, such as anxiety or gravity, is a construct.
Free will	The idea that human beings are capable of freely making choices or decisions is free will.

Go to **Cram101.com** for the Practice Tests for this Chapter.

Learning	Learning is a relatively permanent change in behavior that results from experience. Thus, to attribute a behavioral change to learning, the change must be relatively permanent and must result from experience.
Anatomy	Anatomy is the branch of biology that deals with the structure and organization of living things. It can be divided into animal anatomy (zootomy) and plant anatomy (phytonomy). Major branches of anatomy include comparative anatomy, histology, and human anatomy.
Determinism	Determinism is the philosophical proposition that every event, including human cognition and action, is causally determined by an unbroken chain of prior occurrences.
Watson	Watson, the father of behaviorism, developed the term "Behaviorism" as a name for his proposal to revolutionize the study of human psychology in order to put it on a firm experimental footing.
Walden Two	Walden Two, a novel by B.F. Skinner, describes a fictional community designed around behavioral principles. The fictional utopian commune thrives on a level of productivity and happiness of its citizens far in advance of that in the outside world due to it's practice of scientific social planning and the use of operant conditioning in the raising of children.
Pavlov	Pavlov first described the phenomenon now known as classical conditioning in experiments with dogs.
Ideology	An ideology can be thought of as a comprehensive vision, as a way of looking at things, as in common sense and several philosophical tendencies, or a set of ideas proposed by the dominant class of a society to all members of this society.
Physiology	The study of the functions and activities of living cells, tissues, and organs and of the physical and chemical phenomena involved is referred to as physiology.
Depression	In everyday language depression refers to any downturn in mood, which may be relatively transitory and perhaps due to something trivial. This is differentiated from Clinical depression which is marked by symptoms that last two weeks or more and are so severe that they interfere with daily living.
Society	The social sciences use the term society to mean a group of people that form a semi-closed (or semi-open) social system, in which most interactions are with other individuals belonging to the group.
Intellectually gifted	Intellectually gifted refers to having an IQ score above 130; about 2 to 4 percent of the population.
Creative thinking	Creative thinking is a mental process involving the generation of new ideas or concepts, or new associations between existing ideas or concepts. From a scientific point of view, the products of are usually considered to have both originality and appropriateness.
Emotion	An emotion is a mental states that arise spontaneously, rather than through conscious effort. They are often accompanied by physiological changes.
Utopian	An ideal vision of society is a utopian society.
Catharsis	Catharsis has been adopted by modern psychotherapy as the act of giving expression to deep emotions often associated with events in the individuals past which have never before been adequately expressed.
Shaping	The concept of reinforcing successive, increasingly accurate approximations to a target behavior is called shaping. The target behavior is broken down into a hierarchy of elemental steps, each step more sophisticated then the last. By successively reinforcing each of the the elemental steps, a form of differential reinforcement, until that step is learned while extinguishing the step below, the target behavior is gradually achieved.

Go to **Cram101.com** for the Practice Tests for this Chapter.

Beyond Freedom and Dignity	Beyond Freedom and Dignity is a book-length essay written by B. F. Skinner. The book argued that entrenched belief in free will and the moral autonomy of the individual hindered the prospect of building a happier and better organized society through the use of scientific techniques for modifying behavior.
American Psychological Association	The American Psychological Association is a professional organization representing psychology in the US. The mission statement is to "advance psychology as a science and profession and as a means of promoting health, education , and human welfare".
William James	Functionalism as a psychology developed out of Pragmatism as a philosophy: To find the meaning of an idea, you have to look at its consequences. This led William James and his students towards an emphasis on cause and effect, prediction and control, and observation of environment and behavior, over the careful introspection of the Structuralists.
Thorndike	Thorndike worked in animal behavior and the learning process leading to the theory of connectionism. Among his most famous contributions were his research on cats escaping from puzzle boxes, and his formulation of the Law of Effect.
Law of effect	The law of effect is a principle of psychology described by Edward Thorndike in 1898. It holds that responses to stimuli that produce a satisfying or pleasant effect in a particular situation are more likely to occur again in the situation. Conversely, responses that produce a discomforting or unpleasant effect are less likely to occur again in the situation
Introspection	Introspection is the self report or consideration of one's own thoughts, perceptions and mental processes. Classic introspection was done through trained observers.
Consciousness	The awareness of the sensations, thoughts, and feelings being experienced at a given moment is called consciousness.
Stimulus	A change in an environmental condition that elicits a response is a stimulus.
Habit	A habit is a response that has become completely separated from its eliciting stimulus. Early learning theorists used the term to describe S-R associations, however not all S-R associations become a habit, rather many are extinguished after reinforcement is withdrawn.
Motives	Needs or desires that energize and direct behavior toward a goal are motives.
Instinct	Instinct is the word used to describe inherent dispositions towards particular actions. They are generally an inherited pattern of responses or reactions to certain kinds of situations.
Motivation	In psychology, motivation is the driving force (desire) behind all actions of an organism.
Variable	A variable refers to a measurable factor, characteristic, or attribute of an individual or a system.
Deprivation	Deprivation, is the loss or withholding of normal stimulation, nutrition, comfort, love, and so forth; a condition of lacking. The level of stimulation is less than what is required.
Empirical	Empirical means the use of working hypotheses which are capable of being disproved using observation or experiment.
Attitude	An enduring mental representation of a person, place, or thing that evokes an emotional response and related behavior is called attitude.
Plato	According to Plato, people must come equipped with most of their knowledge and need only hints and contemplation to complete it. Plato suggested that the brain is the mechanism of mental processes and that one gained knowledge by reflecting on the contents of one's mind.
Wisdom	Wisdom is the ability to make correct judgments and decisions. It is an intangible quality gained through experience. Whether or not something is wise is determined in a pragmatic sense by its popularity, how long it has been around, and its ability to predict against

Go to **Cram101.com** for the Practice Tests for this Chapter.

future events.

Aristotle	Aristotle can be credited with the development of the first theory of learning. He concluded that ideas were generated in consciousness based on four principlesof association: contiguity, similarity, contrast, and succession. In contrast to Plato, he believed that knowledge derived from sensory experience and was not inherited.
Conditioning	Conditioning describes the process by which behaviors can be learned or modified through interaction with the environment.
Operant Conditioning	A simple form of learning in which an organism learns to engage in behavior because it is reinforced is referred to as operant conditioning. The consequences of a behavior produce changes in the probability of the behavior's occurence.
Respondent Conditioning	Respondent conditioning refers to behavior that is elicited involuntarily as a reaction to a stimulus. Respondent behavior is identical to classical conditioning UC to UR relationships.
Classical conditioning	Classical conditioning is a simple form of learning in which an organism comes to associate or anticipate events. A neutral stimulus comes to evoke the response usually evoked by a natural or unconditioned stimulus by being paired repeatedly with the unconditioned stimulus.
Reinforcement	In operant conditioning, reinforcement is any change in an environment that (a) occurs after the behavior, (b) seems to make that behavior re-occur more often in the future and (c) that reoccurence of behavior must be the result of the change.
Unconditioned response	An Unconditioned Response is the response elicited to an unconditioned stimulus. It is a natural, automatic response.
Unconditioned stimulus	In classical conditioning, an unconditioned stimulus elicits a response from an organism prior to conditioning. It is a naturally occurring stimulus and a naturally occurring response..
Conditioned response	A conditioned response is the response to a stimulus that occurs when an animal has learned to associate the stimulus with a certain positive or negative effect.
Reflex	A simple, involuntary response to a stimulus is referred to as reflex. Reflex actions originate at the spinal cord rather than the brain.
Pupil	In the eye, the pupil is the opening in the middle of the iris. It appears black because most of the light entering it is absorbed by the tissues inside the eye. The size of the pupil is controlled by involuntary contraction and dilation of the iris, in order to regulate the intensity of light entering the eye. This is known as the pupillary reflex.
Species	Species refers to a reproductively isolated breeding population.
Simple reflexes	Simple reflexes refers to Piaget's first sensorimotor substage, which corresponds to the first month after birth. In this substage, the basic means of coordinating sensation and action is through reflexive behaviors, such as rooting and sucking, which the infant has at birth.
Little Albert	The Little Albert experiment was an experiment showing empirical evidence of classical conditioning in children. The actual experiment with Little Albert on conditioned fear involved exposing the child to a loud sound while being presented with a white rat.
Conditioned stimulus	A previously neutral stimulus that elicits the conditioned response because of being repeatedly paired with a stimulus that naturally elicited that response, is called a conditioned stimulus.
Successive approximations	In operant conditioning, a series of behaviors that gradually become more similar to a target behavior are called successive approximations.

Go to **Cram101.com** for the Practice Tests for this Chapter.

Go to **Cram101.com** for the Practice Tests for this Chapter.
And, **NEVER** highlight a book again!

Operant behavior	Operant behavior is simply emitted by an organism, that is, all organisms are inherently active, emitting responses that operate in the environment. Unlike respondent behavior, which is dependent on the stimulus that preceded it, operant behavior is a function of its consequences.
Discrimination	In Learning theory, discrimination refers the ability to distinguish between a conditioned stimulus and other stimuli. It can be brought about by extensive training or differential reinforcement. In social terms, it is the denial of privileges to a person or a group on the basis of prejudice.
Stimulus generalization	When animals are trained to respond to a single stimulus and test stimuli are introduced that differ from the training stimulus, generally along a single dimension, the systematic decrement in responding typically found has been called the gradient of stimulus generalization.
Generalization	In conditioning, the tendency for a conditioned response to be evoked by stimuli that are similar to the stimulus to which the response was conditioned is a generalization. The greater the similarity among the stimuli, the greater the probability of generalization.
Identical elements	Thorndike's theory suggests that transfer of learning depends upon the presence of identical elements in the original and new learning situations; i.e., transfer is always specific, never general. In later versions of the theory, the concept of "belongingness" was introduced; connections are more readily established if the person perceives that stimuli or responses go together.
Reinforcer	In operant conditioning, a reinforcer is any stimulus that increases the probability that a preceding behavior will occur again. In Classical Conditioning, the unconditioned stimulus (US) is the reinforcer.
Positive reinforcement	In positive reinforcement, a stimulus is added and the rate of responding increases.
Negative reinforcement	During negative reinforcement, a stimulus is removed and the frequency of the behavior or response increases.
Aversive stimulus	A stimulus that elicits pain, fear, or avoidance is an aversive stimulus.
Anxiety	Anxiety is a complex combination of the feeling of fear, apprehension and worry often accompanied by physical sensations such as palpitations, chest pain and/or shortness of breath.
Punishment	Punishment is the addtion of a stimulus that reduces the frequency of a response, or the removal of a stimulus that results in a reduction of the response.
Negative reinforcer	Negative reinforcer is a reinforcer that when removed increases the frequency of an response.
Guilt	Guilt describes many concepts related to a negative emotion or condition caused by actions which are believed to be, morally wrong. According to Freud, the avoidance of guilt is the basis for moral behavior.
Generalized reinforcer	Generalized reinforcer refers to any secondary reinforcer that has been paired with several different primary reinforcers.
Conditioned reinforcer	A conditioned reinforcer is a stimulus or situation that has acquired reinforcing power after being paired in the environment with an unconditioned reinforcer or an earlier conditioned reinforcer.
Secondary	A conditioned reinforcer, sometimes called a secondary reinforcer, is a stimulus or situation

Go to **Cram101.com** for the Practice Tests for this Chapter.
And, **NEVER** highlight a book again!

Reinforcer	that has acquired reinforcing power after being paired in the environment with an unconditioned reinforcer or an earlier conditioned reinforcer.
Primary Reinforcer	Any stimulus whose reinforcing effect is immediate and not a function of previous experience is a primary reinforcer (eg, food, water, warmth).
Attention	Attention is the cognitive process of selectively concentrating on one thing while ignoring other things. Psychologists have labeled three types of attention: sustained attention, selective attention, and divided attention.
Reinforcement value	The reinforcement value is the strength of the rate of responding or the intensity of the response.
Schedules of Reinforcement	Different combinations of frequency and timing of reinforcement following a behavior are referred to as schedules of reinforcement. They are either continuous (the behavior is reinforced each time it occurs) or intermittent (the behavior is reinforced only on certain occasions).
Positive reinforcer	In operant conditioning, a stimulus that is presented after a response that increases the likelihood that the response will be repeated is a positive reinforcer.
Extinction	In operant extinction, if no reinforcement is delivered after the response, gradually the behavior will no longer occur in the presence of the stimulus. The process is more rapid following continuous reinforcement rather than after partial reinforcement. In Classical Conditioning, repeated presentations of the CS without being followed by the US results in the extinction of the CS.
Intermittent reinforcement	In an intermittent reinforcement schedule, a designated response is reinforced only some of the time.
Schedule of reinforcement	A schedule of reinforcement is either continuous (the behavior is reinforced each time it occurs) or intermittent (the behavior is reinforced only on certain occasions).
Behavior modification	Behavior Modification is a technique of altering an individual's reactions to stimuli through positive reinforcement and the extinction of maladaptive behavior.
Genetics	Genetics is the science of genes, heredity, and the variation of organisms.
Natural selection	Natural selection is a process by which biological populations are altered over time, as a result of the propagation of heritable traits that affect the capacity of individual organisms to survive and reproduce.
Rooting reflex	The rooting reflex is a newborn's built-in reaction that occurs when the infant's cheek is stroked or the side of the mouth is touched. In response, the infant turns its head toward the side that was touched in an apparent effort to find something to suck.
Obesity	The state of being more than 20 percent above the average weight for a person of one's height is called obesity.
Evolution	Commonly used to refer to gradual change, evolution is the change in the frequency of alleles within a population from one generation to the next. This change may be caused by different mechanisms, including natural selection, genetic drift, or changes in population (gene flow).
Verbal Behavior	Verbal Behavior is a book written by B.F. Skinner in which the author presents his ideas on language. For Skinner, speech, along with other forms of communication, was simply a behavior. Skinner argued that each act of speech is an inevitable consequence of the speaker's current environment and his behavioral and sensory history.
Mental processes	The thoughts, feelings, and motives that each of us experiences privately but that cannot be observed directly are called mental processes.

Go to **Cram101.com** for the Practice Tests for this Chapter.

Creativity	Creativity is the ability to think about something in novel and unusual ways and come up with unique solutions to problems. It involves divergent thinking, having many solutions or views to a problem.
Cognition	The intellectual processes through which information is obtained, transformed, stored, retrieved, and otherwise used is cognition.
Problem solving	An attempt to find an appropriate way of attaining a goal when the goal is not readily available is called problem solving.
Overt behavior	An action or response that is directly observable and measurable is an overt behavior.
Evolutionary theory	Evolutionary theory is concerned with heritable variability rather than behavioral variations. Natural selection requirements: (1) natural variability within a species must exist, (2) only some individual differences are heritable, and (3) natural selection only takes place when there is an interaction between the inborn attributes of organisms and the environment in which they live.
Mutation	Mutation is a permanent, sometimes transmissible (if the change is to a germ cell) change to the genetic material (usually DNA or RNA) of a cell. They can be caused by copying errors in the genetic material during cell division and by exposure to radiation, chemicals, or viruses, or can occur deliberately under cellular control during the processes such as meiosis or hypermutation.
Free choice	Free choice refers to the ability to freely make choices that are not controlled by genetics, learning, or unconscious forces.
Blocking	If the one of the two members of a compound stimulus fails to produce the CR due to an earlier conditioning of the other member of the compound stimulus, blocking has occurred.
Psychotherapy	Psychotherapy is a set of techniques based on psychological principles intended to improve mental health, emotional or behavioral issues. Commonly psychotherapy involves a therapist and client(s), who discuss their issues in an effort to discover what they are and how they can solve them.
Striving for superiority	According to Adler, the universal drive to adapt, improve oneself, and master life's challenges is referred to as striving for superiority.
Collective unconscious	Collective unconscious is a term of analytical psychology, originally coined by Carl Jung. It refers to that part of a person's unconscious which is common to all human beings. It contains archetypes, which are forms or symbols that are manifested by all people in all cultures.
Affect	A subjective feeling or emotional tone often accompanied by bodily expressions noticeable to others is called affect.
Behavior therapy	Behavior therapy refers to the systematic application of the principles of learning to direct modification of a client's problem behaviors.
Stimulant	A stimulant is a drug which increases the activity of the sympathetic nervous system and produces a sense of euphoria or awakeness.
Cocaine	Cocaine is a crystalline tropane alkaloid that is obtained from the leaves of the coca plant. It is a stimulant of the central nervous system and an appetite suppressant, creating what has been described as a euphoric sense of happiness and increased energy.
Nicotine	Nicotine is an organic compound, an alkaloid found naturally throughout the tobacco plant, with a high concentration in the leaves. It is a potent nerve poison and is included in many insecticides. In lower concentrations, the substance is a stimulant and is one of the main factors leading to the pleasure and habit-forming qualities of tobacco smoking.

Go to **Cram101.com** for the Practice Tests for this Chapter.

Placebo	Placebo refers to a bogus treatment that has the appearance of being genuine.
Baseline	Measure of a particular behavior or process taken before the introduction of the independent variable or treatment is called the baseline.
Individual differences	Individual differences psychology studies the ways in which individual people differ in their behavior. This is distinguished from other aspects of psychology in that although psychology is ostensibly a study of individuals, modern psychologists invariably study groups.
Sedative	A sedative is a drug that depresses the central nervous system (CNS), which causes calmness, relaxation, reduction of anxiety, sleepiness, slowed breathing, slurred speech, staggering gait, poor judgment, and slow, uncertain reflexes.
Questionnaire	A self-report method of data collection or clinical assessment method in which the individual being studied checks off items on a printed list, answers multiple-choice questions, or writes out answers to essay questions aimed at producing a selfdescription is called questionnaire.
Neurotransmitter	A neurotransmitter is a chemical that is used to relay, amplify and modulate electrical signals between a neurons and another cell.
Dopamine	Dopamine is critical to the way the brain controls our movements and is a crucial part of the basal ganglia motor loop. It is commonly associated with the 'pleasure system' of the brain, providing feelings of enjoyment and reinforcement to motivate us to do, or continue doing, certain activities.
Introvert	Introvert refers to a person whose attention is focused inward; a shy, reserved, timid person.
Hypothesis	A specific statement about behavior or mental processes that is testable through research is a hypothesis.
Personality trait	According to the Diagnostic and Statistical Manual of the American Psychiatric Association, a personality trait is a "prominent aspect of personality that is exhibited in a wide range of important social and personal contexts. ...".
Descriptive research	Descriptive research is also known as statistical research. It describes data about the population being studied. Descriptive reseach answers the following questions: who, what, where, when and how.
Analogy	An analogy is a comparison between two different things, in order to highlight some form of similarity. Analogy is the cognitive process of transferring information from a particular subject to another particular subject.
Illusion	An illusion is a distortion of a sensory perception.
Autonomy	Autonomy is the condition of something that does not depend on anything else.
Heredity	Heredity is the transfer of characteristics from parent to offspring through their genes.
Adaptation	Adaptation is a lowering of sensitivity to a stimulus following prolonged exposure to that stimulus. Behavioral adaptations are special ways a particular organism behaves to survive in its natural habitat.
Teleology	While science investigates natural laws and phenomena, Philosophical naturalism and teleology investigate the existence or non-existence of an organizing principle behind those natural laws and phenonema. Philosophical naturalism asserts that there are no such principles. Teleology asserts that there are.
Causation	Causation concerns the time order relationship between two or more objects such that if a specific antecedent condition occurs the same consequent must always follow.

Maslow	Maslow is mostly noted today for his proposal of a hierarchy of human needs which he often presented as a pyramid. Maslow was an instrumental player in the formation of the humanistic movement, also known as the third force in psychology.
Reinforcement contingencies	The circumstances or rules that determine whether responses lead to the presentation of reinforcers are referred to as reinforcement contingencies. Skinner defined culture as a set of reinforcement contingencies.

Go to **Cram101.com** for the Practice Tests for this Chapter.

Theories	Theories are logically self-consistent models or frameworks describing the behavior of a certain natural or social phenomenon. They are broad explanations and predictions concerning phenomena of interest.
Shyness	A tendency to avoid others plus uneasiness and strain when socializing is called shyness.
Social cognitive theory	Social cognitive theory defines human behavior as a triadic, dynamic, and reciprocal interaction of personal factors, behavior, and the environment. Response consequences of a behavior are used to form expectations of behavioral outcomes. It is the ability to form these expectations that give humans the capability to predict the outcomes of their behavior, before the behavior is performed.
Phobia	A persistent, irrational fear of an object, situation, or activity that the person feels compelled to avoid is referred to as a phobia.
Learning	Learning is a relatively permanent change in behavior that results from experience. Thus, to attribute a behavioral change to learning, the change must be relatively permanent and must result from experience.
Observational learning	The acquisition of knowledge and skills through the observation of others rather than by means of direct experience is observational learning. Four major processes are thought to influence the observational learning: attentional, retentional, behavioral production, and motivational.
Depression	In everyday language depression refers to any downturn in mood, which may be relatively transitory and perhaps due to something trivial. This is differentiated from Clinical depression which is marked by symptoms that last two weeks or more and are so severe that they interfere with daily living.
Bandura	Bandura is best known for his work on social learning theory or Social Cognitivism. His famous Bobo doll experiment illustrated that people learn from observing others.
Causation	Causation concerns the time order relationship between two or more objects such that if a specific antecendent condition occurs the same consequent must always follow.
Personality	Personality refers to the pattern of enduring characteristics that differentiates a person, the patterns of behaviors that make each individual unique.
Vicarious learning	Vicarious learning is learning without specific reinforcement for one's behavior. It is learning by observing others.
Skinner	Skinner conducted research on shaping behavior through positive and negative reinforcement, and demonstrated operant conditioning, a technique which he developed in contrast with classical conditioning.
Reinforcement	In operant conditioning, reinforcement is any change in an environment that (a) occurs after the behavior, (b) seems to make that behavior re-occur more often in the future and (c) that reoccurence of behavior must be the result of the change.
Psychopathology	Psychopathology refers to the field concerned with the nature and development of mental disorders.
Clinical psychology	Clinical psychology is involved in the diagnosis, assessment, and treatment of patients with mental or behavioral disorders, and conducts research in these various areas.
Rorschach	The Rorschach inkblot test is a method of psychological evaluation. It is a projective test associated with the Freudian school of thought. Psychologists use this test to try to probe the unconscious minds of their patients.
Psychotherapy	Psychotherapy is a set of techniques based on psychological principles intended to improve mental health, emotional or behavioral issues. Commonly psychotherapy involves a therapist

and client(s), who discuss their issues in an effort to discover what they are and how they can solve them.

Social learning	Social learning is learning that occurs as a function of observing, retaining and replicating behavior observed in others. Although social learning can occur at any stage in life, it is thought to be particularly important during childhood, particularly as authority becomes important.
Social learning theory	Social learning theory explains the process of gender typing in terms of observation, imitation, and role playing .
Society	The social sciences use the term society to mean a group of people that form a semi-closed (or semi-open) social system, in which most interactions are with other individuals belonging to the group.
American Psychological Association	The American Psychological Association is a professional organization representing psychology in the US. The mission statement is to "advance psychology as a science and profession and as a means of promoting health, education , and human welfare".
Attitude	An enduring mental representation of a person, place, or thing that evokes an emotional response and related behavior is called attitude.
Necessary condition	A circumstance required for a particular phenomenon to occur is a necessary condition if and only if the condition does not occur in the absense of the circumstance.
Punishment	Punishment is the addtion of a stimulus that reduces the frequency of a response, or the removal of a stimulus that results in a reduction of the response.
Modeling	A type of behavior learned through observation of others demonstrating the same behavior is modeling.
Motivation	In psychology, motivation is the driving force (desire) behind all actions of an organism.
Attention	Attention is the cognitive process of selectively concentrating on one thing while ignoring other things. Psychologists have labeled three types of attention: sustained attention, selective attention, and divided attention.
Behavioral Production	Behavioral production or motor reproduction is another process in observational learning. The observer must be able to reproduce the model's behavior. The observer must learn and posses the physical capabilities of the modeled behavior.
Coding	In senation, coding is the process by which information about the quality and quantity of a stimulus is preserved in the pattern of action potentials sent through sensory neurons to the central nervous system.
Acquisition	Acquisition is the process of adapting to the environment, learning or becoming conditioned. In classical conditoning terms, it is the initial learning of the stimulus response link, which involves a neutral stimulus being associated with a unconditioned stimulus and becoming a conditioned stimulus.
Variable	A variable refers to a measurable factor, characteristic, or attribute of an individual or a system.
Cognition	The intellectual processes through which information is obtained, transformed, stored, retrieved, and otherwise used is cognition.
Reciprocal Determinism	Bandura's term for the social-cognitive view that people influence their environment just as their environment influences them is reciprocal determinism.
Determinism	Determinism is the philosophical proposition that every event, including human cognition and action, is causally determined by an unbroken chain of prior occurrences.

Instinct	Instinct is the word used to describe inherent dispositions towards particular actions. They are generally an inherited pattern of responses or reactions to certain kinds of situations.
Physical attractiveness	Physical attractiveness is the perception of an individual as physically beautiful by other people.
Conditioning	Conditioning describes the process by which behaviors can be learned or modified through interaction with the environment.
Maslow	Maslow is mostly noted today for his proposal of a hierarchy of human needs which he often presented as a pyramid. Maslow was an instrumental player in the formation of the humanistic movement, also known as the third force in psychology.
Scheme	According to Piaget, a hypothetical mental structure that permits the classification and organization of new information is called a scheme.
Agentic	"The core features of agency enable people to play a part in their self-development, adaptation, and self-renewal with changing times, " Bandura's agentic perspective of social cognitive theory. The person is active in the process.
Homunculus	Homunculus is a term used in a number of ways to describe systems that are thought of as being run by a "little man" inside. For instance, the homunculus continues to be considered as one of the major theories on the origin of consciousness, that there is a part in the brain whose purpose is to be "you".
Intentionality	Brentano defined intentionality as the main characteristic of "psychical phenomena," by which they could be distinguished from "physical phenomena.". Every mental phenomenon, every psychological act has a content, is directed at an object (the intentional object).
Forethought	Forethought is a person's capability to motivate themselves and guide their actions anticipatorily. Stimuli are not automatically linked to the response by contiguity. Instead, previous experiences create expectations of the outcome that will occur as a result of performing a behavior, before the behavior is performed.
Reciprocity	Reciprocity, in interpersonal attraction, is the tendency to return feelings and attitudes that are expressed about us.
Postulates	Postulates are general statements about behavior that cannot be directly verified. They are used to generate theorems which can be tested.
Affect	A subjective feeling or emotional tone often accompanied by bodily expressions noticeable to others is called affect.
Habit	A habit is a response that has become completely separated from its eliciting stimulus. Early learning theorists used the term to describe S-R associations, however not all S-R associations become a habit, rather many are extinguished after reinforcement is withdrawn.
Heroin	Heroin is widely and illegally used as a powerful and addictive drug producing intense euphoria, which often disappears with increasing tolerance. Heroin is a semi-synthetic opioid. It is the 3,6-diacetyl derivative of morphine and is synthesised from it by acetylation.
Predisposition	Predisposition refers to an inclination or diathesis to respond in a certain way, either inborn or acquired. In abnormal psychology, it is a factor that lowers the ability to withstand stress and inclines the individual toward pathology.
Anxiety	Anxiety is a complex combination of the feeling of fear, apprehension and worry often accompanied by physical sensations such as palpitations, chest pain and/or shortness of breath.
Apathy	Apathy is the lack of emotion, motivation, or enthusiasm. Apathy is a psychological term for

a state of indifference — where an individual is unresponsive or "indifferent" to aspects of emotional, social, or physical life. Clinical apathy is considered to be at an elevated level, while a moderate level might be considered depression, and an extreme level could be diagnosed as a dissociative disorder.

Emotion	An emotion is a mental states that arise spontaneously, rather than through conscious effort. They are often accompanied by physiological changes.
Acute	Acute means sudden, sharp, and abrupt. Usually short in duration.
Arousal	Arousal is a physiological and psychological state involving the activation of the reticular activating system in the brain stem, the autonomic nervous system and the endocrine system, leading to increased heart rate and blood pressure and a condition of alertness and readiness to respond.
Incentive	An incentive is what is expected once a behavior is performed. An incentive acts as a reinforcer.
Cognitive restructuring	Cognitive restructuring refers to any behavior therapy procedure that attempts to alter the manner in which a client thinks about life so that he or she changes overt behavior and emotions.
Homosexual	Homosexual refers to a sexual orientation characterized by aesthetic attraction, romantic love, and sexual desire exclusively for members of the same sex or gender identity.
Socioeconomic	Socioeconomic pertains to the study of the social and economic impacts of any product or service offering, market intervention or other activity on an economy as a whole and on the companies, organization and individuals who are its main economic actors.
Chronic	Chronic refers to a relatively long duration, usually more than a few months.
Generalization	In conditioning, the tendency for a conditioned response to be evoked by stimuli that are similar to the stimulus to which the response was conditioned is a generalization. The greater the similarity among the stimuli, the greater the probability of generalization.
Rape	Rape is a crime where the victim is forced into sexual activity, in particular sexual penetration, against his or her will.
Negative reinforcement	During negative reinforcement, a stimulus is removed and the frequency of the behavior or response increases.
Positive reinforcement	In positive reinforcement, a stimulus is added and the rate of responding increases.
Experimental group	Experimental group refers to any group receiving a treatment effect in an experiment.
Bobo doll	The Bobo doll experiment was conducted by Bandura to study aggressive patterns of behavior. One of the experiment's conclusions was that people can learn through vicarious reinforcement.
Control group	A group that does not receive the treatment effect in an experiment is referred to as the control group or sometimes as the comparison group.
Cognitive learning	Higher-level learning involving thinking, knowing, understanding, and anticipation is cognitive learning.
Alcoholic	An alcoholic is dependent on alcohol as characterized by craving, loss of control, physical dependence and withdrawal symptoms, and tolerance.
Alcoholism	A disorder that involves long-term, repeated, uncontrolled, compulsive, and excessive use of alcoholic beverages and that impairs the drinker's health and work and social relationships

Go to **Cram101.com** for the Practice Tests for this Chapter.

is called alcoholism.

Cognitive therapy	Cognitive therapy is a kind of psychotherapy used to treat depression, anxiety disorders, phobias, and other forms of mental disorder. It involves recognizing distorted thinking and learning how to replace it with more realistic thoughts and actions.
Extinction	In operant extinction, if no reinforcement is delivered after the response, gradually the behavior will no longer occur in the presence of the stimulus. The process is more rapid following continuous reinforcement rather than after partial reinforcement. In Classical Conditioning, repeated presentations of the CS without being followed by the US results in the extinction of the CS.
Systematic desensitization	Systematic desensitization refers to Wolpe's behavioral fear-reduction technique in which a hierarchy of fear-evoking stimuli are presented while the person remains relaxed. The fear-evoking stimuli thereby become associated with muscle relaxation.
Desensitization	Desensitization refers to the type of sensory or behavioral adaptation in which we become less sensitive to constant stimuli.
Wolpe	Wolpe is best known for applying classical conditioning principles to the treatment of phobias, called systematic desensitization. Any "neutral" stimulus, simple or complex that happens to make an impact on an individual at about the time that a fear reaction is evoked acquires the ability to evoke fear subsequently. An acquired CS-CR relationship should be extinguishable.
Kagan	The work of Kagan supports the concept of an inborn, biologically based temperamental predisposition to severe anxiety.
Reasoning	Reasoning is the act of using reason to derive a conclusion from certain premises. There are two main methods to reach a conclusion,deductive reasoning and inductive reasoning.
Trait	An enduring personality characteristic that tends to lead to certain behaviors is called a trait. The term trait also means a genetically inherited feature of an organism.
Questionnaire	A self-report method of data collection or clinical assessment method in which the individual being studied checks off items on a printed list, answers multiple-choice questions, or writes out answers to essay questions aimed at producing a selfdescription is called questionnaire.
Neuroticism	Eysenck's use of the term neuroticism (or Emotional Stability) was proposed as the dimension describing individual differences in the predisposition towards neurotic disorder.
Gender difference	A gender difference is a disparity between genders involving quality or quantity. Though some gender differences are controversial, they are not to be confused with sexist stereotypes.
Learning disability	A learning disability exists when there is a significant discrepancy between one's ability and achievement.
Pons	The pons is a knob on the brain stem. It is part of the autonomic nervous system, and relays sensory information between the cerebellum and cerebrum. Some theories posit that it has a role in dreaming.
Aptitude test	A test designed to predict a person's ability in a particular area or line of work is called an aptitude test.
Role model	A person who serves as a positive example of desirable behavior is referred to as a role model.
Falsifiability	According to Popper the extent to which a scientific assertion is amenable to systematic probes, any one of which could negate the scientist's expectations is referred to as falsifiability.

Empirical	Empirical means the use of working hypotheses which are capable of being disproved using observation or experiment.
Parsimony	In science, parsimony is preference for the least complicated explanation for an observation. This is generally regarded as good when judging hypotheses. Occam's Razor also states the "principle of parsimony".
Trial and error	Trial and error is an approach to problem solving in which one solution after another is tried in no particular order until an answer is found.
Plasticity	The capacity for modification and change is referred to as plasticity.
Striving for superiority	According to Adler, the universal drive to adapt, improve oneself, and master life's challenges is referred to as striving for superiority.
Prejudice	Prejudice in general, implies coming to a judgment on the subject before learning where the preponderance of the evidence actually lies, or formation of a judgement without direct experience.
Teleology	While science investigates natural laws and phenomena, Philosophical naturalism and teleology investigate the existence or non-existence of an organizing principle behind those natural laws and phenonema. Philosophical naturalism asserts that there are no such principles. Teleology asserts that there are.
Dichotomy	A dichotomy is the division of a proposition into two parts which are both mutually exclusive – i.e. both cannot be simultaneously true – and jointly exhaustive – i.e. they cover the full range of possible outcomes. They are often contrasting and spoken of as "opposites".
Social influence	Social influence is when the actions or thoughts of individual(s) are changed by other individual(s). Peer pressure is an example of social influence.
Individual differences	Individual differences psychology studies the ways in which individual people differ in their behavior. This is distinguished from other aspects of psychology in that although psychology is ostensibly a study of individuals, modern psychologists invariably study groups.

Go to **Cram101.com** for the Practice Tests for this Chapter.

Rotter	Rotter focused on the application of social learning theory (SLT) to clinical psychology. She introduced the ideas of learning from generalized expectancies of reinforcement and internal/ external locus of control (self-initiated change versus change influenced by others). According to Rotter, health outcomes could be improved by the development of a sense of personal control over one's life.
Theories	Theories are logically self-consistent models or frameworks describing the behavior of a certain natural or social phenomenon. They are broad explanations and predictions concerning phenomena of interest.
Social learning	Social learning is learning that occurs as a function of observing, retaining and replicating behavior observed in others. Although social learning can occur at any stage in life, it is thought to be particularly important during childhood, particularly as authority becomes important.
Social learning theory	Social learning theory explains the process of gender typing in terms of observation, imitation, and role playing .
Learning	Learning is a relatively permanent change in behavior that results from experience. Thus, to attribute a behavioral change to learning, the change must be relatively permanent and must result from experience.
Mischel	Mischel is known for his cognitive social learning model of personality that focuses on the specific cognitive variables that mediate the manner in which new experiences affect the individual.
Reinforcement	In operant conditioning, reinforcement is any change in an environment that (a) occurs after the behavior, (b) seems to make that behavior re-occur more often in the future and (c) that reoccurence of behavior must be the result of the change.
Social cognitive theory	Social cognitive theory defines human behavior as a triadic, dynamic, and reciprocal interaction of personal factors, behavior, and the environment. Response consequences of a behavior are used to form expectations of behavioral outcomes. It is the ability to form these expectations that give humans the capability to predict the outcomes of their behavior, before the behavior is performed.
Personality	Personality refers to the pattern of enduring characteristics that differentiates a person, the patterns of behaviors that make each individual unique.
Depression	In everyday language depression refers to any downturn in mood, which may be relatively transitory and perhaps due to something trivial. This is differentiated from Clinical depression which is marked by symptoms that last two weeks or more and are so severe that they interfere with daily living.
Psychopathology	Psychopathology refers to the field concerned with the nature and development of mental disorders.
Human nature	Human nature is the fundamental nature and substance of humans, as well as the range of human behavior that is believed to be invariant over long periods of time and across very different cultural contexts.
Adler	Adler argued that human personality could be explained teleologically, separate strands dominated by the guiding purpose of the individual's unconscious self ideal to convert feelings of inferiority to superiority (or rather completeness). The desires of the self ideal were countered by social and ethical demands.
Society	The social sciences use the term society to mean a group of people that form a semi-closed (or semi-open) social system, in which most interactions are with other individuals belonging to the group.

Individual psychology	Alfred Adler's individual psychology approach views people as motivated by purposes and goals, being creators of their own lives .
Clinical psychology	Clinical psychology is involved in the diagnosis, assessment, and treatment of patients with mental or behavioral disorders, and conducts research in these various areas.
Clinical psychologist	A psychologist, usually with a Ph.D, whose training is in the diagnosis, treatment, or research of psychological and behavioral disorders is a clinical psychologist.
Personality psychology	Personality psychology is a branch of psychology which studies personality and individual difference processes. One emphasis in personality psychology is on trying to create a coherent picture of a person and all his or her major psychological processes.
Interpersonal trust	A personality dimension involving one's belief that other people are trustworthy, dependable, and reliable or that they are untrustworthy, undependable, and unreliable is called interpersonal trust.
American Psychological Association	The American Psychological Association is a professional organization representing psychology in the US. The mission statement is to "advance psychology as a science and profession and as a means of promoting health, education , and human welfare".
Variable	A variable refers to a measurable factor, characteristic, or attribute of an individual or a system.
Reinforcement value	The reinforcement value is the strength of the rate of responding or the intensity of the response.
Psychological situation	A psychological situation refers to situation as it is perceived and interpreted by an individual, not necessarily as it exists objectively.
Positive reinforcement	In positive reinforcement, a stimulus is added and the rate of responding increases.
Skinner	Skinner conducted research on shaping behavior through positive and negative reinforcement, and demonstrated operant conditioning, a technique which he developed in contrast with classical conditioning.
Perception	Perception is the process of acquiring, interpreting, selecting, and organizing sensory information.
Variance	The degree to which scores differ among individuals in a distribution of scores is the variance.
Cognition	The intellectual processes through which information is obtained, transformed, stored, retrieved, and otherwise used is cognition.
Trait	An enduring personality characteristic that tends to lead to certain behaviors is called a trait. The term trait also means a genetically inherited feature of an organism.
Shaping	The concept of reinforcing successive, increasingly accurate approximations to a target behavior is called shaping. The target behavior is broken down into a hierarchy of elemental steps, each step more sophisticated then the last. By successively reinforcing each of the the elemental steps, a form of differential reinforcement, until that step is learned while extinguishing the step below, the target behavior is gradually achieved.
Generalization	In conditioning, the tendency for a conditioned response to be evoked by stimuli that are similar to the stimulus to which the response was conditioned is a generalization. The greater the similarity among the stimuli, the greater the probability of generalization.
Deprivation	Deprivation, is the loss or withholding of normal stimulation, nutrition, comfort, love, and so forth; a condition of lacking. The level of stimulation is less than what is required.

Go to **Cram101.com** for the Practice Tests for this Chapter.

Arousal	Arousal is a physiological and psychological state involving the activation of the reticular activating system in the brain stem, the autonomic nervous system and the endocrine system, leading to increased heart rate and blood pressure and a condition of alertness and readiness to respond.
Socioeconomic	Socioeconomic pertains to the study of the social and economic impacts of any product or service offering, market intervention or other activity on an economy as a whole and on the companies, organization and individuals who are its main economic actors.
Socioeconomic Status	A family's socioeconomic status is based on family income, parental education level, parental occupation, and social status in the community. Those with high status often have more success in preparing their children for school because they have access to a wide range of resources.
Reinforcer	In operant conditioning, a reinforcer is any stimulus that increases the probability that a preceding behavior will occur again. In Classical Conditioning, the unconditioned stimulus (US) is the reinforcer.
Locus of control	The place to which an individual attributes control over the receiving of reinforcers -either inside or outside the self is referred to as locus of control.
Correlation	A statistical technique for determining the degree of association between two or more variables is referred to as correlation.
Apathy	Apathy is the lack of emotion, motivation, or enthusiasm. Apathy is a psychological term for a state of indifference — where an individual is unresponsive or "indifferent" to aspects of emotional, social, or physical life. Clinical apathy is considered to be at an elevated level, while a moderate level might be considered depression, and an extreme level could be diagnosed as a dissociative disorder.
Punishment	Punishment is the addtion of a stimulus that reduces the frequency of a response, or the removal of a stimulus that results in a reduction of the response.
Individual differences	Individual differences psychology studies the ways in which individual people differ in their behavior. This is distinguished from other aspects of psychology in that although psychology is ostensibly a study of individuals, modern psychologists invariably study groups.
Social psychology	Social psychology is the study of the nature and causes of human social behavior, with an emphasis on how people think towards each other and how they relate to each other.
Maladaptive	In psychology, a behavior or trait is adaptive when it helps an individual adjust and function well within their social environment. A maladaptive behavior or trait is counterproductive to the individual.
Psychotherapy	Psychotherapy is a set of techniques based on psychological principles intended to improve mental health, emotional or behavioral issues. Commonly psychotherapy involves a therapist and client(s), who discuss their issues in an effort to discover what they are and how they can solve them.
Context	In Psychology, context refers to the background stimuli that accompany some kind of foreground event.
Pragmatism	Pragmatism is characterized by the insistence on consequences, utility and practicality as vital components of truth. Pragmatism objects to the view that human concepts and intellect represent reality, and therefore stands in opposition to both formalist and rationalist schools of philosophy.
Repression	A defense mechanism, repression involves moving thoughts unacceptable to the ego into the unconscious, where they cannot be easily accessed.

Go to **Cram101.com** for the Practice Tests for this Chapter.

Assertiveness	Assertiveness basically means the ability to express your thoughts and feelings in a way that clearly states your needs and keeps the lines of communication open with the other.
Motives	Needs or desires that energize and direct behavior toward a goal are motives.
Attitude	An enduring mental representation of a person, place, or thing that evokes an emotional response and related behavior is called attitude.
Allport	Allport was a trait theorist. Those traits he believed to predominate a person's personality were called central traits. Traits such that one could be indentifed by the trait, were referred to as cardinal traits. Central traits and cardinal traits are influenced by environmental factors.
Trait theory	According to trait theory, personality can be broken down into a limited number of traits, which are present in each individual to a greater or lesser degree. This approach is highly compatible with the quantitative psychometric approach to personality testing.
Humanistic	Humanistic refers to any system of thought focused on subjective experience and human problems and potentials.
Psychoanalytic	Freud's theory that unconscious forces act as determinants of personality is called psychoanalytic theory. The theory is a developmental theory characterized by critical stages of development.
Psychoanalytic theory	Psychoanalytic theory is a general term for approaches to psychoanalysis which attempt to provide a conceptual framework more-or-less independent of clinical practice rather than based on empirical analysis of clinical cases.
Empirical	Empirical means the use of working hypotheses which are capable of being disproved using observation or experiment.
Empirical evidence	Facts or information based on direct observation or experience are referred to as empirical evidence.
George Kelly	George Kelly developed his major contribution to the psychology of personality, The Psychology of Personal Constructs in 1955 and achieved immediate international recognition. He worked in clinical school psychology, developing a program of traveling clinics which also served as a training ground for his students.
Research design	A research design tests a hypothesis. The basic typess are: descriptive, correlational, and experimental.
Construct	A generalized concept, such as anxiety or gravity, is a construct.
Bandura	Bandura is best known for his work on social learning theory or Social Cognitivism. His famous Bobo doll experiment illustrated that people learn from observing others.
Cognitive psychology	Cognitive psychology is the psychological science which studies the mental processes that are hypothesised to underlie behavior. This covers a broad range of research domains, examining questions about the workings of memory, attention, perception, knowledge representation, reasoning, creativity and problem solving.
Standardized test	An oral or written assessment for which an individual receives a score indicating how the individual reponded relative to a previously tested large sample of others is referred to as a standardized test.
Personality trait	According to the Diagnostic and Statistical Manual of the American Psychiatric Association, a personality trait is a "prominent aspect of personality that is exhibited in a wide range of important social and personal contexts. ...".
Individuality	According to Cooper, individuality consists of two dimensions: self-assertion and

Go to Cram101.com for the Practice Tests for this Chapter.

	separateness.
Hans Eysenck	Hans Eysenck using Factor Analysis concluded that all human traits can be broken down into two distinct categories: 1. Extroversion-Introversion, 2. Neuroticism. He called these categories Supertraits.
Variability	Statistically, variability refers to how much the scores in a distribution spread out, away from the mean.
Conscientiou-ness	Conscientiousness is one of the dimensions of the five-factor model of personality and individual differences involving being organized, thorough, and reliable as opposed to careless, negligent, and unreliable.
Affective	Affective is the way people react emotionally, their ability to feel another living thing's pain or joy.
Stimulus	A change in an environmental condition that elicits a response is a stimulus.
Feedback	Feedback refers to information returned to a person about the effects a response has had.
Encoding	Encoding refers to interpreting; transforming; modifying information so that it can be placed in memory. It is the first stage of information processing.
Affect	A subjective feeling or emotional tone often accompanied by bodily expressions noticeable to others is called affect.
Conditioning	Conditioning describes the process by which behaviors can be learned or modified through interaction with the environment.
Classical conditioning	Classical conditioning is a simple form of learning in which an organism comes to associate or anticipate events. A neutral stimulus comes to evoke the response usually evoked by a natural or unconditioned stimulus by being paired repeatedly with the unconditioned stimulus.
Emotion	An emotion is a mental states that arise spontaneously, rather than through conscious effort. They are often accompanied by physiological changes.
Countercondi-ioning	The process of eliminating a classically conditioned response by pairing the CS with an unconditioned stimulus for a response that is stronger than the conditioned response and that cannot occur at the same time as the CR is called counterconditioning.
Selective attention	Selective attention is a type of attention which involves focusing on a specific aspect of a scene while ignoring other aspects.
Attention	Attention is the cognitive process of selectively concentrating on one thing while ignoring other things. Psychologists have labeled three types of attention: sustained attention, selective attention, and divided attention.
Suicide	Suicide behavior is rare in childhood but escalates in adolescence. The suicide rate increases in a linear fashion from adolescence through late adulthood.
Suicidal ideation	Suicidal ideation refers to having serious thoughts about committing suicide.
Beck	Beck was initially trained as a psychoanalyst and conducted research on the psychoanalytic treatment of depression. With out the strong ability to collect data to this end, he began exploring cognitive approaches to treatment and originated cognitive behavior therapy.
Gender difference	A gender difference is a disparity between genders involving quality or quantity. Though some gender differences are controversial, they are not to be confused with sexist stereotypes.
Counselor	A counselor is a mental health professional who specializes in helping people with problems not involving serious mental disorders.

Go to **Cram101.com** for the Practice Tests for this Chapter.

Catastrophizing	Catastrophizing refers to interpreting negative life events in pessimistic, global terms. People who consistently explain bad events as catastrophes are found to have a shortened life span.
Stereotype	A stereotype is considered to be a group concept, held by one social group about another. They are often used in a negative or prejudicial sense and are frequently used to justify certain discriminatory behaviors. This allows powerful social groups to legitimize and protect their dominant position
Hue	A hue refers to the gradation of color within the optical spectrum, or visible spectrum, of light. Hue may also refer to a particular color within this spectrum, as defined by its dominant wavelength, or the central tendency of its combined wavelengths.
Free choice	Free choice refers to the ability to freely make choices that are not controlled by genetics, learning, or unconscious forces.
Social influence	Social influence is when the actions or thoughts of individual(s) are changed by other individual(s). Peer pressure is an example of social influence.
Predisposition	Predisposition refers to an inclination or diathesis to respond in a certain way, either inborn or acquired. In abnormal psychology, it is a factor that lowers the ability to withstand stress and inclines the individual toward pathology.
Reinforcement Theory	Reinforcement theory holds that reinforcers can control behavior. The definition has two main components: Contingency, where the occurrence of the reinforcer depends on the occurrence of the learner's response, and Rate of Responding, where the reinforcer serves to increase the learner's rate of responding.

Theories	Theories are logically self-consistent models or frameworks describing the behavior of a certain natural or social phenomenon. They are broad explanations and predictions concerning phenomena of interest.
Psychotherapy	Psychotherapy is a set of techniques based on psychological principles intended to improve mental health, emotional or behavioral issues. Commonly psychotherapy involves a therapist and client(s), who discuss their issues in an effort to discover what they are and how they can solve them.
Learning	Learning is a relatively permanent change in behavior that results from experience. Thus, to attribute a behavioral change to learning, the change must be relatively permanent and must result from experience.
George Kelly	George Kelly developed his major contribution to the psychology of personality, The Psychology of Personal Constructs in 1955 and achieved immediate international recognition. He worked in clinical school psychology, developing a program of traveling clinics which also served as a training ground for his students.
Construct	A generalized concept, such as anxiety or gravity, is a construct.
Personality	Personality refers to the pattern of enduring characteristics that differentiates a person, the patterns of behaviors that make each individual unique.
Pathology	Pathology is the study of the processes underlying disease and other forms of illness, harmful abnormality, or dysfunction.
Physiological psychology	Physiological psychology refers to the study of the physiological mechanisms, in the brain and elsewhere, that mediate behavior and psychological experiences.
Depression	In everyday language depression refers to any downturn in mood, which may be relatively transitory and perhaps due to something trivial. This is differentiated from Clinical depression which is marked by symptoms that last two weeks or more and are so severe that they interfere with daily living.
Rotter	Rotter focused on the application of social learning theory (SLT) to clinical psychology. She introduced the ideas of learning from generalized expectancies of reinforcement and internal/external locus of control (self-initiated change versus change influenced by others). According to Rotter, health outcomes could be improved by the development of a sense of personal control over one's life.
Maslow	Maslow is mostly noted today for his proposal of a hierarchy of human needs which he often presented as a pyramid. Maslow was an instrumental player in the formation of the humanistic movement, also known as the third force in psychology.
Clinical psychology	Clinical psychology is involved in the diagnosis, assessment, and treatment of patients with mental or behavioral disorders, and conducts research in these various areas.
Perception	Perception is the process of acquiring, interpreting, selecting, and organizing sensory information.
Scientific observation	An empirical investigation that is structured to answer questions about the world is a scientific observation.
Carl Rogers	Carl Rogers was instrumental in the development of non-directive psychotherapy, also known as "client-centered" psychotherapy. Rogers' basic tenets were unconditional positive regard, genuineness, and empathic understanding, with each demonstrated by the counselor.
Adler	Adler argued that human personality could be explained teleologically, separate strands dominated by the guiding purpose of the individual's unconscious self ideal to convert feelings of inferiority to superiority (or rather completeness). The desires of the self

Go to **Cram101.com** for the Practice Tests for this Chapter.

Go to **Cram101.com** for the Practice Tests for this Chapter.
And, **NEVER** highlight a book again!

	ideal were countered by social and ethical demands.
Psychoanalysis	Psychoanalysis refers to the school of psychology that emphasizes the importance of unconscious motives and conflicts as determinants of human behavior. It was Freud's method of exploring human personality.
Seduction theory	Freud believed that all hyseria was traceable to sexual seduction and abuse. This theory, known as the seduction theory, he later modified and replaced with a psychoanalytic alternative, hysteria.
Oedipus complex	The Oedipus complex is a concept developed by Sigmund Freud to explain the maturation of the infant boy through identification with the father and desire for the mother.
Psychoanalytic	Freud's theory that unconscious forces act as determinants of personality is called psychoanalytic theory. The theory is a developmental theory characterized by critical stages of development.
Psychoanalytic theory	Psychoanalytic theory is a general term for approaches to psychoanalysis which attempt to provide a conceptual framework more-or-less independent of clinical practice rather than based on empirical analysis of clinical cases.
Hypothesis	A specific statement about behavior or mental processes that is testable through research is a hypothesis.
Context	In Psychology, context refers to the background stimuli that accompany some kind of foreground event.
Society	The social sciences use the term society to mean a group of people that form a semi-closed (or semi-open) social system, in which most interactions are with other individuals belonging to the group.
Individual differences	Individual differences psychology studies the ways in which individual people differ in their behavior. This is distinguished from other aspects of psychology in that although psychology is ostensibly a study of individuals, modern psychologists invariably study groups.
Individuality	According to Cooper, individuality consists of two dimensions: self-assertion and separateness.
Identical twins	Identical twins occur when a single egg is fertilized to form one zygote (monozygotic) but the zygote then divides into two separate embryos. The two embryos develop into foetuses sharing the same womb. Monozygotic twins are genetically identical unless there has been a mutation in development, and they are almost always the same gender.
Superordinate	A hypernym is a word whose extension includes the extension of the word of which it is a hypernym. A word that is more generic or broad than another given word. Another term for a hypernym is a superordinate.
Dichotomy	A dichotomy is the division of a proposition into two parts which are both mutually exclusive – i.e. both cannot be simultaneously true – and jointly exhaustive – i.e. they cover the full range of possible outcomes. They are often contrasting and spoken of as "opposites".
Attention	Attention is the cognitive process of selectively concentrating on one thing while ignoring other things. Psychologists have labeled three types of attention: sustained attention, selective attention, and divided attention.
Modulation	Modulation is the process of varying a carrier signal, typically a sinusoidal signal, in order to use that signal to convey information.
Adaptation	Adaptation is a lowering of sensitivity to a stimulus following prolonged exposure to that stimulus. Behavioral adaptations are special ways a particular organism behaves to survive in its natural habitat.

Go to **Cram101.com** for the Practice Tests for this Chapter.

Trait	An enduring personality characteristic that tends to lead to certain behaviors is called a trait. The term trait also means a genetically inherited feature of an organism.
Mischel	Mischel is known for his cognitive social learning model of personality that focuses on the specific cognitive variables that mediate the manner in which new experiences affect the individual.
Psychological disorder	Mental processes and/or behavior patterns that cause emotional distress and/or substantial impairment in functioning is a psychological disorder.
Diagnostic and Statistical Manual of Mental Disorders	The Diagnostic and Statistical Manual of Mental Disorders, published by the American Psychiatric Association, is the handbook used most often in diagnosing mental disorders in the United States and internationally.
Mental disorder	Mental disorder refers to a disturbance in a person's emotions, drives, thought processes, or behavior that involves serious and relatively prolonged distress and/or impairment in ability to function, is not simply a normal response to some event or set of events in the person's environment.
Anxiety	Anxiety is a complex combination of the feeling of fear, apprehension and worry often accompanied by physical sensations such as palpitations, chest pain and/or shortness of breath.
Guilt	Guilt describes many concepts related to a negative emotion or condition caused by actions which are believed to be, morally wrong. According to Freud, the avoidance of guilt is the basis for moral behavior.
Attitude	An enduring mental representation of a person, place, or thing that evokes an emotional response and related behavior is called attitude.
Stages	Stages represent relatively discrete periods of time in which functioning is qualitatively different from functioning at other periods.
Repertory Grid	Repertory Grid is an interviewing technique that complements the Theory of Personal Constructs. It aims to get people to talk about their construct system, and to identify the repertoire of constructs an individual typically uses to make sense of particular situations.
Validity	The extent to which a test measures what it is intended to measure is called validity.
Reliability	Reliability means the extent to which a test produces a consistent , reproducible score .
Personality psychology	Personality psychology is a branch of psychology which studies personality and individual difference processes. One emphasis in personality psychology is on trying to create a coherent picture of a person and all his or her major psychological processes.
Empirical	Empirical means the use of working hypotheses which are capable of being disproved using observation or experiment.
Schema	Schema refers to a way of mentally representing the world, such as a belief or an expectation, that can influence perception of persons, objects, and situations.
Social cognition	Social cognition is the name for both a branch of psychology that studies the cognitive processes involved in social interaction, and an umbrella term for the processes themselves. It uses the tools and assumptions of cognitive psychology to study how people understand themselves and others in society and social situations.
Cognition	The intellectual processes through which information is obtained, transformed, stored, retrieved, and otherwise used is cognition.

Go to **Cram101.com** for the Practice Tests for this Chapter.

Stereotype	A stereotype is considered to be a group concept, held by one social group about another. They are often used in a negative or prejudicial sense and are frequently used to justify certain discriminatory behaviors. This allows powerful social groups to legitimize and protect their dominant position
Bias	A bias is a prejudice in a general or specific sense, usually in the sense for having a preference to one particular point of view or ideological perspective.
Social schemas	Organized clusters of ideas about categories of social events and people are referred to as social schemas.
Mental Representation	Stage six of the sensorimotor substages, Mental representation, 18 months to 2 years, marks the beginnings of insight, or true creativity. This marks the passage into unique thought in Piaget's later three areas of development.
Questionnaire	A self-report method of data collection or clinical assessment method in which the individual being studied checks off items on a printed list, answers multiple-choice questions, or writes out answers to essay questions aimed at producing a selfdescription is called questionnaire.
Gender stereotypes	Broad categories that reflect our impressions and beliefs about typical females and males are referred to as gender stereotypes.
Idiographic	An idiographic investigation studies the characteristics of an individual in depth.
Watson	Watson, the father of behaviorism, developed the term "Behaviorism" as a name for his proposal to revolutionize the study of human psychology in order to put it on a firm experimental footing.
Social self	A collective identity that includes interpersonal relationships plus aspects of identity derived from membership in larger, less personal groups based on race, ethnicity, and culture is called the social self.
Likert scale	A Likert scale is a type of psychometric scale often used in questionnaires. It asks respondents to specify their level of agreement to each of a list of statements. It is a bipolar scaling method, measuring either positive and negative response to a statement.
Parsimony	In science, parsimony is preference for the least complicated explanation for an observation. This is generally regarded as good when judging hypotheses. Occam's Razor also states the "principle of parsimony".
Motivation	In psychology, motivation is the driving force (desire) behind all actions of an organism.
Human nature	Human nature is the fundamental nature and substance of humans, as well as the range of human behavior that is believed to be invariant over long periods of time and across very different cultural contexts.
Free choice	Free choice refers to the ability to freely make choices that are not controlled by genetics, learning, or unconscious forces.
Determinism	Determinism is the philosophical proposition that every event, including human cognition and action, is causally determined by an unbroken chain of prior occurrences.
Social influence	Social influence is when the actions or thoughts of individual(s) are changed by other individual(s). Peer pressure is an example of social influence.

CPSIA information can be obtained at www.ICGtesting.com
Printed in the USA
BVOW01s0749311213

340574BV00002B/13/P